T0065468

Alzheimer's The Disease That Destroys The Mind

Jeanette Cox

authorHOUSE·

AuthorHouse™
1663 Liberty Drive
Bloomington, IN 47403
www.authorhouse.com
Phone: 833-262-8899

Published by AuthorHouse 06/16/2021

ISBN: 978-1-6655-2332-5 (sc)
ISBN: 978-1-6655-2331-8 (e)

CONTENTS

PROJECT OBJECTIVE

When I was eight years old, my parents, three sisters, and I moved from North Philadelphia to South Philadelphia, Pennsylvania. We moved into one of the newly built four housing project buildings, with twelve floors. We lived on the fifth floor, Apartment 5E. Our parents let us play with the other children. Suppose a kid was standing alone, I would always stop playing with a group of kids, walk over to the kid who was alone and start playing with him/her until he/she seems comfortable walking over to play with the rest of us. I always felt the need to make someone happy. I also love helping the elderly carry their groceries, laundry, or running errands when my parents allowed me. With that feeling of excitement and their acknowledgment at that early age, I felt I was doing something great for the world.

When I was fourteen, our family moved to West Philadelphia. St. Bernard Street right off 50th and Market Street. I recalled running an errand for my mom to 52nd and Market Street. As I was returning home, I spotted this older woman walking slow. I ran up to her and asked, "are you okay?" She looked up at me and said, "yes. I'm fine. I'm just walking slow and thinking about my daughters." Our conversation was so impressive that we both were making each other laugh. She told me her name, Ms. Zella. She was 72 years old. I said my name, and that I'm 15 years old. She continues her conversation, laughing. I enjoyed her so much, and I asked her if she would like to meet my mother.

My mother was her daughters' age. She said she would love to. So I took her home and introduced her to my mother; Ms. Zella would make periodic visits to our family.

She was always welcome. My mother said she reminded her of her mother. Ms. Zella and I stayed in communication during my college years. After college, I would drive to Ms. Zella's apartment and run errands for her. I met one of her daughters, who told me that her mother spoke very highly of me. I responded and said to her that her mom is like one of my girlfriends. We talked about anything and everything. Long story short, Ms. Zella and I remained friends until she passed. I was in my mid-twenties.

When I graduated from college with a Bachelor's degree in Social Science and a minor in history, I applied for Social Worker positions but was never successful. I believe my destiny was elsewhere. I needed a job, so I became a substitute teacher. I worked at the Philadelphia School District and loved my job, taking various jobs working with elementary to secondary schools.

One day, I was assigned to a special education middle school class—an emotional support class of six boys and one girl. The first day was challenging. However, I loved the challenge. Sounds crazy, right, yet, I loved it. The principal asked me to come back the next day. At the end of the week, the principal spoke to me again to ask if I could stay until they could find an appointed teacher. All their prior teachers quit because they could not control the class. He said, "on the other hand, you work with the students well." I said yes, but only on one condition—academic will be ¾ of the school day, while the remaining part of the day we will play basketball because the students could not sit that long, they needed to move around. The principal consented. I taught the class for the next three months using the model¾ academic of day and ¼ playing basketball. A process to release tension and built-up negative emotions. That class and the principal inspired me to go back to school to get my Master In Education and specialize in Special Education. I graduated with my Master's degree in June 1982.

Caregiving is my destiny from a child to an adult. Helping others always made me very happy. I also love to see others comfortable and content as well.
This book will share my personal experience in Caregiving. I was caring for an Alzheimer's patient who happens to be my husband. In this book,

I hope to bring awareness and the heartbreaking truth of Alzheimer's Disease.

I'm giving an understanding to the reader about caregiving. The struggles families and friends go through caring for your loved one and making sure proper services are in place. Medical care, insurance, daycare/extended care, wearing adequate clothing. Suppose you are caring for your loved one at home, ensure your home is safe, for example, doors and window locks, protection from the stove, etc. Simultaneously, caring for your health, finances, sustaining your life, and well-being while caring for your loved one.

** September 2019

The World Alzheimer Report 2019: *Attitudes toward dementia.* The report was launched on September 20, 2019, the day before World Alzheimer's Day. You can access the information at www.alz.co.uk/worldreport2019.

The report combines analysis of the world's largest survey on attitudes to dementia and expert essays and case studies from around the globe. It concludes by providing recommendations for governments, agencies, civil society, and policy-makers to improve people living with dementia, their carers, and loved ones across the globe. The seminal piece of research is motivated by the belief that individuals with dementia should access support and services without fear of stigmatization.

INTRODUCTION

My parents were members of the church as a young couple. They joined in 1945. Three years later, my oldest sister was born. Four and a half years later, my twin sister and I were born. Four and a half years after, my youngest sister was born. My sisters and I grew up in this church. Every Sunday, that's where you would find the Cox family, and sometimes, weekdays for bible study and Friday night service.

I met John (Jay) Benjamin Beckwith at church. Jay and his wife joined in the 1980s. He became a deacon, well-liked and respected. Jay's wife became very ill, and he was her caregiver until she passed. My mother and oldest sister introduced us, and we got married in May 1992.

Your daily life seems to be going well until you notice little changes with your husband, losing keys, his wallet, money, cannot remember his work schedule, and it goes on and on for the simple daily tasks. Instantly, I thought his diabetes medication needed to be adjusted. So, I made an appointment with the family physician, from there to the neurologist. To my surprise, it all goes downhill from that point. In March 2002, my husband, fifty-seven years old, was diagnosed. The End of The Middle Stages Of Alzheimer's. Three months after Jay's diagnosis, I started my journal to help me keep level-headed because of the changes my husband was going through so quickly. A year after his diagnosis, I knew I must share my story, and I will write a book one day.

In preparation to write my book in 2019, I contacted the Alzheimer's Association, Maryland Chapter, the state I presently live, to interview other caregivers of Alzheimer's/Dementia patients and get their permission to use their various experiences as caregivers in this book. Throughout my book, you will read about four other caregivers' stories about caring for their loved ones. Mr. Edgar H. Parker, Mrs. Florence Nightingale(asked me not to use her real name), Ms. Peggy S. Jackson, and Mrs. Betty J Whitaker. My story as the caregiver for my husband.

CHAPTER 1

His Regular Days to Transitional Days. His Thoughts Are Confusing Him

Regular workdays are Monday through Friday as a forklift operator. Jay's uniforms are neatly pressed, which he retrieves from his closet. Jay's clothes are nicely and faithfully washed on Saturdays. Jay was always very neat, from every dress shirt or suit socks, whether dress or work clothes. He makes sure to prepare for the upcoming work week.

Monday morning, Jay is up at five in the morning preparing to leave and get to work by seven. He takes the back roads of Cheltenham Township, which cuts his travel time down fifteen to twenty minutes, depending on the weather.

Wednesday nights are date nights for Jay and me. We go to any restaurant we have a particular taste for. We both love to go to the Outback restaurant. On Friday nights, we order takeout for the whole family. Sometimes it's a deli near his job or wherever the kids have a desire to eat that day.

Saturdays, Jay and I get up at about eight to prepare to go to the food market. The grocery food list has accumulated over the last week of the various foods, toiletries, and cleaning products needed. Jay would stop for gas just before we started shopping. His routine was always spot-on every time we went grocery shopping.

When we return home after grocery shopping, Jay would take the groceries into the house. I would unload the groceries and put them away. Meanwhile, Jay would gather up the dirty laundry, go to the laundry room, and start loading the washing machine. Following that chore, he would help me clean the house. Anything and everything that was needed, Jay got it done. He completed chores like yard work, plumbing, light electrical work, painting, and maintaining the cars. He knew how to keep the light needed jobs around the house done.

Saturday nights, he prepared for Sunday church services, Sunday's dinner, and deciding his attire for church. If potato salad or fruit salad were on Sunday's menu, Jay would prepare them. He always was more than happy to help me in the kitchen.

Sunday mornings, everyone's up by eight and preparing for church services. I would go downstairs and prepare breakfast and be done by nine-thirty, then we are all upstairs to finish dressing and out of the house by ten-fifteen. We all arrived at church ten minutes before eleven. That's the time church service starts. Jay maintained his duties as a deacon at church while he could.

Our vacations consist of visiting his family in Florida, Disney World, and various beaches, Cocoa Beach in Florida, Virginia Beach, and Ocean City, Maryland, and a family cruise to Mexico.

Medical Changes Are Trickling In

In 1992, I recalled our honeymoon. We decided to vacation in Montego Bay, Jamaica. We both were excited, especially Jay, because his brother-in-law-had a family there. Jay really wanted to visit them because he had not seen them for a while. I booked various tours. We visited his family for dinner in their home. We were constantly on the go. I noticed Jay was always thirsty and tired, and he wanted to sleep instead of going on tour. I said to him, "we did not come all this way for you to sleep." He explained that he did not know why he was so tired. So, we missed a few tours because he wanted to sleep. I realized something was physically completely wrong, but we were out of the country. I could not wait to get back home to make an appointment for Jay to see the family doctor.

When we returned to the states, I immediately made the appointment. After the complete physical, Jay's blood tests reveal he had type one or two diabetes. Our family doctor recommended seeing an endocrinologist. So the appointment was made. The endocrinologist put Jay on a strict diet. I was very happy because Jay would eat like a growing adolescent. She prescribes Jay one diabetic pill twice a day, and we had to attend classes once a week for a month. Jay learned how to change his bad eating habits, and I learned how to cook for a person who had diabetes.

I implemented a strategic routine. Jay and I started an exercise routine after work. We would go for long walks, and at various times, I suggested to Jay that we sometimes run instead of just walking. He reluctantly agreed, So sometimes we would walk, and all of a sudden, I just started running. I looked back at Jay, saying to him, "Come on, let's go." He would look at me with this frustrating face and start running. He would complain that he was so tired. My response was, "the more we exercised, the easier it will get. This is for your health and your sharp mind too." Every other day we would exercise, his complaints subsided, and he could see the results. His sugar levels were ranging from 120-175, and not 175 and up.

The next step was monitoring his bad eating habits. I tried very hard working with Jay. It was easy when he was home. But, he would come home from work, and his sugar levels were 275 and up. Sometimes, they rose up to 375. I asked, "What are you doing?" I made sure I purchased healthy foods when we went grocery shopping. He would bring lunch from home to work. I said, "and you agreed on following through with what you were taught in the nutrition classes."

"Well," he said, "I go to the vending machines at work. And sometimes and the guys bring in various cakes, cookies, and donuts to work. They leave them in the lunchroom for everybody."

"Jay," I said, "We have been over this several times already."

3

He replied, "I know, it is so hard for me."

I said to him, "Honey, this is so important for your health. You have to take this seriously, please."

His response, "I know. I will do better."

I realized I had to change my ways to help Jay. I would help him monitor his blood sugar levels by watching him and discuss what was going on with him that particular day. We talked about whether his levels were low or high. This type of discussion made him more conscious of his eating habits.

Jay's blood levels continued to fluctuate. The endocrinologist put him on insulin to better control his diabetes. He took two shots a day, one in the morning and one in the evening. The shots helped a lot, however, he did not like giving himself the insulin shots. He said, "I don't like sticking my finger to get the levels and then giving myself insulin shots in my thigh every day. "So many times, I would take it upon myself to administer the insulin shots.

JAD—Journal of Alzheimer's
Body Weight Has Surprising, Alarming Impact on Brain Function

As your weight goes up, all regions of the brain go down in activity and blood flow, according to the Journal of Alzheimer's Disease. In one of the largest studies linking obesity with brain dysfunction, scientists analyzed over 35,000 functional neuroimaging scans using single-photon emission computerized tomography from more than 17,000 individuals to measure blood flow and brain activity.

The Journal of Alzheimer's (JAD) also states low cerebral blood flow is the number one brain imaging predictor that a person will develop Alzheimer's disease. It is also associated with depression, ADHD, bipolar disorder, schizophrenia, traumatic brain injury, addiction, suicide, and other conditions." This study shows that being overweight or obese seriously impacts brain activity and increases the risk for Alzheimer's disease as well as many other psychiatric and cognitive conditions," explained Daniel G. Amen, MD, the study's lead author and founder of Amen Clinics, one of the leading brain-centered mental health clinics in the United States.

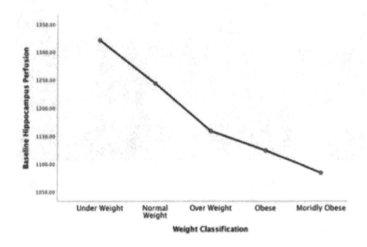

[Caption: Area of obesity-related hypoperfusion in brain regions v vulnerable to Alzheimer's disease: Hippocampus]

Striking patterns of progressively reduced blood flow were found in virtually all regions of the brain across categories of underweight, normal weight, overweight, obesity, and morbid obesity. These were noted while participants were in a resting state as well as while performing a concentrated task. In particular, brain areas noted to be vulnerable to Alzheimer's, the temporal and parietal lobes, hippocampus, posterior cingulate gyrus, and precuneus were found to have reduced blood flow along the spectrum of weight to overweight, obese, and morbidly.

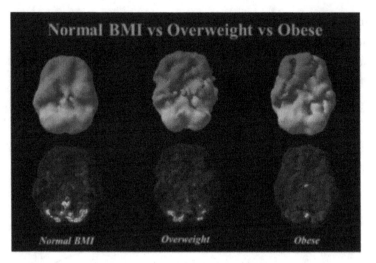

Caption: *3D renderings of blood flow averaged across normal BMI (BMI = 23), overweight (BMI = 29), and obese (BMI = 37) men, each 40 years of age (credit: Amen Clinics)*

Considering the latest statistics that show 72 percent of Americans are overweight and 42 percent of those are obese. This is distressing news for America's mental and cognitive health.

Commenting on this study is George Perry, Ph.D., Editor-in-Chief of the Journal of Disease and Semmes Foundation.

Sleep Apnea and Other Medical Problems

At night I sometimes noticed Jay would stop breathing in his sleep. I would always shake him while he was sleeping so he would start breathing again. That concerned me, so I made an appointment with our family doctor. Our family doctor discovered after various tests that Jay had sleep apnea. He was admitted to the hospital for one-day minor surgery to address his sleep apnea.

HealthDay News in March 2019 reported that millions of Americans are left drowsy each day by sleep apnea, and new research suggests it might also raise their odds for Alzheimer's disease.

Obstructive sleep apnea is a chronic condition that can cause breathing to stop frequently during sleep. Tau, a protein that forms tangles in the brain, is found in people with Alzheimer's. In the study, Carvalho's team looked at 288 people, aged 65 and older, without thinking and memory problems. Each study participant had brain scans to look for tau tangles in the part of the brain involved in memory and perception of time. This area, part of the temporal lobe, is more likely than other brain areas to accumulate tangles.

Also, the researchers asked participants' bed partners if they ever had seen them
experiencing sleep apnea; forty-three participants had such episodes. That finding remained even after the Carvalho team considered other factors linked to tau levels, including age, sex, education, cardiovascular risk factors, and other sleep problems.

"The study has several limitations, the researchers noted. The number of participants was small. No sleep studies were done to confirm apnea. And it was unclear whether participants were already being treated for it, if indicated," Carvalho said. "More study is needed to gauge whether treating sleep apnea prevents tau buildup and reduces dementia risk," he added.

Rebecca Edelmayer, director of scientific engagement at the Alzheimer's Association,
reviewed the study. "These findings align with a lot of the data we've seen with sleep disturbances increasing the risk for cognitive impairment," she said. Though the specific connection between dementia and sleep is unclear, Edelmayer said it might be what stresses the brain. Sleep disturbances may also alter the brain's circadian rhythms—the twenty-four-hour body clock that cycles between alertness and sleepiness.

Edelmayer added that the brain solidifies memories during sleep, and interrupting that process might lead to thinking and memory problems.

"What is known now about the importance of sleep is that good sleep is really important for your overall health."

The study finds are scheduled for presentations at the Academy of Neurology (AAN) meeting in Philadelphia. Research presented at meetings typically considered preliminary until published in a peer-review journal.

Jay was also diagnosed with Hepatitis B. Another appointment was made to have a Liver Biopsy. This time, the doctor let me stay in Jay's room while the biopsy was performed. The doctor told me that I needed to be also tested. My test results came back negative. The doctor explains to both of us about Hepatitis B. And what we needed to do to stay vigilant about hepatitis B. I was very happy with my results. However, my doctor advised me to make sure I am protected. Jay has to wear a condom from now on for my protection until his test is completely clear. I was so shocked about Hepatitis B. I sat down with Jay to discuss how this happens. Jay told me when he was young, he used drugs and used dirty needles. I was lost for words and very upset! This was the first time he ever revealed to me his background. Thank God my test results came back negative.

CHAPTER 2

OMG … Something Noticeably Wrong At Home. His Regular Habits Changing For The Worse

Losing Car/House Keys, Hiding Cash Various Places In The Bedroom

Whenever it was time to go out to run an errand or Jay going to work, Jay could never find his keys. [Losing his keys All-Time raises my concern. Something wrong]. He would be so frustrated when that happens. I suggested putting his keys in the bedroom on his dresser. He was adamant about the care of his car and home and very protective of them both. I would check every day to make sure his keys were on his dresser. Jay would hide money in various places in the bedroom. I would find the money as I would clean our bedroom, and I would ask him why are you putting cash in various places in the bedroom. We had decided to put forty dollars in the safe every two weeks just to have the same cash on the side for emergencies. He could never recall putting the money in those places. I would find it in his closet, his underwear drawer, his dress shirts when I gather them to take to the professional laundry or the corner of his closet. [Signs Of Something Is Wrong] I was concerned, but we were so busy that I just kept it moving.

On Payday Friday's, we would do the household bills together. This time as we were doing the bills, I told Jay to write out a check of a certain amount. I then gave him another bill to write out a check. I noticed he was just standing there staring at the checkbook. I asked, "what's wrong?" He replied, "I forgot how to write out a check," I replied, "what do you mean you forgot how to write out a check." I jumped up from the loveseat in our bedroom and walked over to the dresser where he was standing. He had this puzzled stare[1] I look down at the checkbook in his hand. From that point, I knew something was definitely wrong from the look on his face. All of a sudden, not recalling how to manage the household finances.

So I started a conversation with Jay about his weekly pay. He said that the teller at the bank is always correcting him about filling out the deposit slip. I asked, "Do you recognize the teller since you use the same bank every payday?" He said, "no, I always go to the same teller every week. I can't remember how to fill out the deposit slip." I told Jay that after I get off from work, I will run to our area banking branch and get deposit slips and help him fill them out. I also mentioned direct deposit; all you have to do is to get an authorization form from the bank and give it to the payroll department at the job. I explained the process to him a few times, but it was too complicated for Jay to understand, so I decided to just leave well enough alone. By this time, I was really worried about Jay. Jay always stayed on top of household finances, but all of a sudden, that no longer existed.

Personal Interviews With Other Caregivers

Tuesday, July 23, 2019, I interviewed Mr. Parker, who was the caregiver of his wife, Jean, from the late '90s to early 2000. She retired in 1998. Mr. Parker noticed she was having difficulty with her memory just before her retirement.

Monday, July 29, 2019, I interviewed Mrs. Florence Nightingale. She is the caregiver of her husband. He is 80 years old. Mrs. Nightinale stated that she noticed little changes in her husband's behavior three years ago. Florence

---

[1] **The Alz Stare"-puzzled look, of memory loss. eyes not moving, fixated Author, Jeanette Cox)**

usually visits her hometown in Western Europe every year in March and October. However, my husband's memory is slowly deteriorating, and I don't know if he can travel that far. He forgets little things. I am always there to uphold or fill-in what my husband doesn't remember. Mrs. Nightingale states that she never knows how fast Alzheimer's progresses. She says, "he went out for lunch with a friend the other day, and that evening, he didn't remember he'd been to lunch with him."

Tuesday, July 30, 2019, I interviewed two caregivers, Peggy S. Jackson and Betty J Whitaker. Both are from M.A.R. Alzheimer's Caregivers Support Group in Baltimore, Maryland. Ms. Jackson is the Group Leader, M.A.R. Alzheimer's Caregivers Support Group. She was the caregiver of her mother. Her mother had been an educator. She was a retired teacher and very involved in church, living independently on her own. Ms. Jackson stated that she had difficulty accepting the changes in her mother's behavior. "My mother never spoke loudly. She was a lady like a demir lady, and then I noticed her difference or changes in her behavior. She would speak differently, more adamantly, and more assertively. My mother didn't argue she was just a mild-mannered person. People used to say, "are you sure that she is your mother because I'm so different." I'm outspoken, but my mother was very wise and soft-spoken.

"I began to notice the changes, and the first change I noticed when I visited her one day was when looking at her bills. I could see she had paid her bills twice. She had credits for gas, electric, and telephone bills, and I was saying, "why do you have all these credits on your bill?" I found out when I investigated. She was paying them more than once, the same bills. And that's how I really found out something was wrong." Ms. Jackson states, "another time I visited my mother, she was sitting on the porch. As I came up, it was a warm day, and I smelled burning eggs and smoke. And I opened the door and went into the kitchen. My mother had put boiled eggs on the stove, and the water had boiled out of the pan, and the eggs had burst onto the ceiling. And she was sitting on the porch like nothing had happened. Around that time, I realized that something is definitely wrong."

Mrs. Betty Whitaker is an attendee at M.A.R. Alzheimer's Caregivers Support Group. Ms. Whitaker was the caregiver of her husband for 10 years. She noticed changes in her husband's behavior. Mrs. Whitaker stated that her husband never complained. "He was a real jokester and very active. My husband rides a bike 35 miles a day and likes white water rafting. He also liked skiing in the winter. We always went out West to one of the Wyoming Ski Resort. He doesn't like anything slow like golf."

Between 2001- 2002, Mrs. Whitaker noticed behavior changes. In July of every year, her husband started watching videos of him and his friends skiing, passing between the poles at various speeds. "I said to my husband, "you haven't watched your videos." His friends would video him. He replied, "I'm not going skiing; skiing is the lowest of my life."

"Secondly, "I also noticed he started to complain about his job. My husband was a computer programmer. All of a sudden, he says, "they are not giving me anything to do." He would never complain about his job." She would say to her husband, "whatever they give you, just do it, don't complain." She also noticed her husband lying in bed past the time he was supposed to be at work. Some days, his manager would call and say, "I was just checking in on your husband. He never called to say he was not coming in." Mrs. Whitaker stated her husband always went to work. His manager boasts that she could always depend on her husband. She said, "he comes to work every day and early every day. When we are out of the office luncheons, I know your husband is the only one coming back. He never leaves work early."

Early Simple Test From Home

Google Search: Early Signs of Alzheimer's/Dementia

CHAPTER 3

Is It Jay's Diabetes? Rush For Follow-up Visit. Family Doctor

Immediately I made an appointment with the family doctor explaining to the doctor the various events and difficulties he was having with his thinking process that went on at home that really concerned me. So, the doctor starts to ask Jay questions. Jay, at the moment, seems to be okay until the doctor asked him to remember a pen and pencil. He said, okay. The doctor then asked Jay to count backward from 100. He started to count 100, 99, 98, 97, 96, then he stopped. The doctor told him not to stop and continue. I looked at Jay. He had this dazed look on this face. The same look he had when he couldn't remember how to write checks. Jay could not continue. The doctor asks Jay to recall the two objects she told him before he started counting. He could not recall a pen and pencil. The doctor said to me she is recommending to see the neurologist at Lankenau Medical Office, Dr. Howard Caplan. Mr. Beckwith has signs of early-onset Dementia.

The link between diabetes and Alzheimer's

According to the Mayo Clinic, there's already an established link. There's a lot of research suggesting a connection between diabetes and Alzheimer's, though those connections aren't yet fully understood. Not all studies confirm the connection, but many do suggest that people with diabetes, especially type 2 diabetes, are at higher risk of eventually developing Alzheimer's dementia or other dementias.

Researcher is still unclear on whether taking steps to prevent or control diabetes may help reduce your risk of cognitive decline.[2]

Understanding The Connection

Diabetes can cause several complications, such as damage to your blood vessels. Diabetes is considered a risk factor for vascular dementia. This type of dementia occurs due to brain damage that is often caused by reduced or blocked blood flow of your brain.

Many people with diabetes have brain changes that are hallmarks of both Alzheimer's disease and vascular dementia. Some researchers think that each condition fuels the damage caused by the other.

Ongoing research is aimed at trying to better understand the link between Alzheimer's and diabetes. That link may occur as a result of the complex ways that type 2 diabetes affect the ability of the brain and body tissues to use sugar (glucose) and respond to insulin.

Diabetes may also increase the risk of developing mild cognitive impairment (MCI), a condition in which people experience more thinking (cognitive) and memory problems than are usually present in normal aging. Some research indicates that diabetes may increase the risk of (MCI) worsening to dementia. Mild cognitive impairment may precede or accompany Alzheimer's disease and other types of dementia.

As researchers examine the connections between diabetes and Alzheimer's, they also study potential ways to prevent or treat both diseases. But a recent trial of intranasal insulin showed no benefit.[3]

---

[2] MayoClinic.org 1998-2019 Mayo Foundation For Medical Education and Research
[3] MayoClinic.org. 1998-2019 Mayo Foundation For Medical Education and Research

JAD Journal of
Alzheimer's Disease

Alzheimer's Disease provides insight into the association of blood markers of diabetes with brain beta-amyloid accumulation among older people at risk of dementia. The results suggest a link between Alzheimer's pathology, lower levels of insulin, and lower insulin resistance.

The deposition of beta-amyloid plaques in the brain is known to be one of the key elements of Alzheimer's disease and can begin years or even decades before the disease progresses to the dementia stage. Amyloid accumulation in the brain can be detected by PET scans.

Type 2 diabetes is a known risk factor for cognitive impairment and Alzheimer's disease, but the underlying mechanisms are still unknown. Autopsy studies have found that diabetes is associated with small vessel pathology typical of Alzheimer's disease. Insulin resistance, an indicator of a pre-diabetic state, has been associated with amyloid accumulation in cognitively normal middle-age and late-middle age individuals, but not in the older age groups.

In this study, researchers from the University of Eastern Finland investigated the association of blood markers of diabetes with beta-amyloid accumulation detected in PET scans in older people at risk of dementia. The study population included 41 participants from the Finish Geriatric Intervention Study to Prevent Cognitive Impairment and Disability(Finger). Finger has investigated the cognitive benefits of a multidomain lifestyle intervention for people over 60 who are at risk of cognitive decline.

Results from the study indicated slightly better insulin homeostasis in amyloid positive older individuals at risk of dementia. The findings contrast with earlier findings, possibly due to the fact that this study population was at high risk of cognitive decline. "The results could also suggest that in people with diabetes and vascular pathology, less amyloid accumulation in the brain may be needed to trigger the onset of Alzheimer's dementia," Associate Professor Alina Solomon from the University of Eastern Finland says.

"Interestingly, no association was found for amyloid deposition with fasting glucose levels or HbA1c, which measures the average level of blood sugar."

The new study adds to the growing amount of data on the associations of insulin resistance and diabetes with Alzheimer's disease pathology.

Working with your health care team reduces your risk to prevent diabetes or manage diabetes has been shown an effective strategy to avoid or minimize complications.

Within a week, we were sitting in the neurologist office at Lankenau Medical. Dr. Caplan read our family doctor's notes and ordered a battery of neurological tests for Jay. Jay went through tests that were ordered. The neurology department called us back into his office within two weeks. Dr. Caplan sat us down to explain his tentative diagnosis as Dementia with early signs of onset Alzheimer's Disease. He explains the disease to us thoroughly.

Dr. Caplan mentions that his Mother and Father were also diagnosed with the disease years prior and is the reason why he studied neurological disorders extensively.

After listening to the doctor, I said, "Jay is fairly young to be diagnosed with this type of disease!" He answered that Jay was not his youngest patient. His youngest patient was 32 years old. "Eventually, driving will be too difficult for Mr. Beckwith." I was very surprised and shocked as I continued to listen intensely.

Dr. Caplan prescribed Jay medication to help him with his memory, and he wanted us to get a second opinion from a neurologist at the University Of Pennsylvania by the name of Dr. Murray Grossman, whose practice was totally devoted to Alzheimer's patients. I made an appointment for mid-February 2002.

The Meeting With Dr. Murray Grossman

Jay and I were sitting right outside Dr. Grossman's office, when this middle build man with glasses and a calm pleasant voice opened his door. Mr. and Mrs. Beckwith, please come in. Mr. Beckwith, you sit here, which is in close proximity to his small desk. And Mrs. Beckwith, you can sit over there in that chair. After going over all the information that was sent to him by all your doctors, He said, I would like to administer some neurological tests of my own. In one of the tests, I will be inserting dye into your arm and give you an MRI of the brain and take pictures of your brain activity. There will be a few other tests, and from there, there will be a more complete and accurate diagnosis. However, you will not be able to return to work until all the tests are completed. Jay stood up out of the chair with this angry voice. "What do you mean I can't go back to work! I have to take care of my family." I proceed to explain," Jay, we will be fine. We will work it out. Please, calm down and listen to Dr. Grossman, he is here to help." Jay stood there for about five more seconds. He finally sat down and listened calmly. Dr. Grossman replied, "after all the testing is done, you probably will be able to return to work."

CHAPTER 4

March 5, 2002
The Diagnosis, End Of The
Middle Stage Of Alzheimer's

The Phone Call

Driving to work on a breeze sunny day, about 45 minutes away from my home. Through all the morning traffic, I finally reached the school building. I found a parking space a block away from the school building. As I was parking my car, a call comes in; it was Dr. Grossman. I greeted him with anxious hello. I was very anxious to hear what he had to say. "I have your husband's test results," he said, "your husband is presently at the end of the Middle Stages of Alzheimer's. He will no longer be able to work. I will give you all the necessary documentation you will need for his job. At this point in Dr. Grossman's call, my thoughts were scattered. He continued, "Mrs. Beckwith, you can apply for Social Security Disability for your husband. Social Security should not reject your husband based on our findings. However, if they do, please contact me. I will give you the name of a great attorney that will handle their rejection if need be. Please make an appointment with my secretary as soon as possible, Mrs. Beckwith, I am so sorry. I will speak to you soon."

I was so overwhelmed and in shock. I thought, what does this mean for our family? Tears started to roll down my cheeks. It took me about 15 minutes before I could get out of the car to walk to the school building. All-day at work, I was thinking. How am I going to explain to a 57-year-old man that he is unable to work again? I remembered two months prior, I applied for Mortgage Health Insurance; if something happens and either one could not work, the insurance company would pay our mortgage. Unfortunately, my husband refused to sign up for mortgage insurance. I had no idea Jay was ill at the time.

After work, I rush home. Jay was in the backyard cleaning. I let him know that I was home, and I sat down at the kitchen table. He came in and sat down. He asked me about my day at work, and I told him it was okay. Then I cautiously, in a calm voice, said to him that Dr. Grossman called. Jay looked at me with this nervous expression on his face, he replied, "what did he say." I explained the diagnosis as quickly as I could to him. You will not be able to return to work because of this illness. Please understand that this is the best. You have to retire early. You have over 30 years on the job. Dr. Grossman says that you can apply for Social Security Disability. I held Jay's hand the whole time I was explaining to him my conversation with Dr. Grossman, and fighting my tears back to stay composed in front of Jay. You love working around the house. You always said that you never have enough time to do all the things you would like to do around here, now you can. Jay didn't say a word, he just had this sad look on his face. Again, I repeated, there are so many projects around the house you want to do. Now you can do them. Jay was very handy around the house. He saved us a lot of money not calling contractors because he could do the work himself. He thought about it for a moment, calmed down, and agreed there are many things he can do around the house.

In two weeks, we are sitting in Dr. Grossman's office. He went over all the test results with us and gave me Jay's prescriptions. He asked me if there are any questions. I said no, not at this time. "I am always here for you," he said. I told him that I am gathering all the necessary paperwork to apply for social security disability. Again, Dr. Grossman said, "if you need anything, just contact my secretary." I thank him, and so did Jay. Jay and I headed for the door. Dr. Grossman said to me, "Mrs. Beckwith, get your finances in order!" I thanked him again and walked out of the door. I was thinking to myself; my finances are in order! SO I THOUGHT!

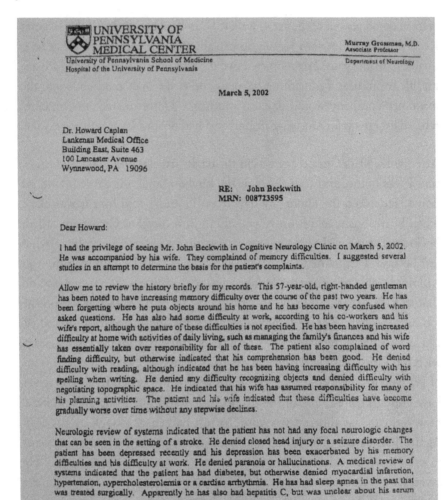

UNIVERSITY OF PENNSYLVANIA MEDICAL CENTER

University of Pennsylvania School of Medicine
Hospital of the University of Pennsylvania

Murray Grossman, M.D.
Associate Professor

Department of Neurology

March 5, 2002

Dr. Howard Caplan
Lankenau Medical Office
Building East, Suite 463
100 Lancaster Avenue
Wynnewood, PA 19096

RE: John Beckwith
MRN: 008723595

Dear Howard:

I had the privilege of seeing Mr. John Beckwith in Cognitive Neurology Clinic on March 5, 2002. He was accompanied by his wife. They complained of memory difficulties. I suggested several studies in an attempt to determine the basis for the patient's complaints.

Allow me to review the history briefly for my records. This 57-year-old, right-handed gentleman has been noted to have increasing memory difficulty over the course of the past two years. He has been forgetting where he puts objects around his home and he has become very confused when asked questions. He has also had some difficulty at work, according to his co-workers and his wife's report, although the nature of these difficulties is not specified. He has been having increased difficulty at home with activities of daily living, such as managing the family's finances and his wife has essentially taken over responsibility for all of these. The patient also complained of word finding difficulty, but otherwise indicated that his comprehension has been good. He denied difficulty with reading, although indicated that he has been having increasing difficulty with his spelling when writing. He denied any difficulty recognizing objects and denied difficulty with negotiating topographic space. He indicated that his wife has assumed responsibility for many of his planning activities. The patient and his wife indicated that these difficulties have become gradually worse over time without any stepwise declines.

Neurologic review of systems indicated that the patient has not had any focal neurologic changes that can be seen in the setting of a stroke. He denied closed head injury or a seizure disorder. The patient has been depressed recently and his depression has been exacerbated by his memory difficulties and his difficulty at work. He denied paranoia or hallucinations. A medical review of systems indicated that the patient has had diabetes, but otherwise denied myocardial infarction, hypertension, hypercholesterolemia or a cardiac arrhythmia. He has had sleep apnea in the past that was treated surgically. Apparently he has also had hepatitis C, but was unclear about his serum

3 W. Gates Building • 3400 Spruce Street • Philadelphia, PA 19104-4283 • 215-662-3361 • Fax: 215-349-8464
email: mgrossma@mail.med.upenn.edu
UNIVERSITY OF PENNSYLVANIA HEALTH SYSTEM

Murray Grossman, M D. Associate Professor
Department of Neurology
University of Pennsylvania Medical Center
School of Medicine
Hospital of the University of Pennsylvania

enzyme level. He denied any genitourinary complaints. He complained of right shoulder arthritis. He denied any endocrinologic complaints, although he has had parathyroid gland excised. He has had diabetes. He denied any hematologic complaints. The patient never smoked cigarettes and consumed alcohol remotely. In his work as a forklift operator, he has had no exposure to environmental toxins. He denied any medication allergies. His family has a significant history of memory difficulty in a brother and a sister of unclear etiology. His current medication regimen has included Reminyl 8 mg bid, Glucovance 5/500, two tabs bid, Humulin N 15 units q a.m. and Zoloft 50 mg q d.

The patient appeared well medically. Examination of the head, eyes, ears, nose and throat revealed a normocephalic cranial vault that was atraumatic. There was no temporal artery nodularity no sinus tenderness that I could detect. There were no neck masses. Funduscopic examination revealed sharp disc margins bilaterally.

Neurologic evaluation revealed the patient's mental status to be alert, and he was oriented to person, partially to place and partially to time. Evaluation of attention revealed the patient's ability to maintain vigilance during the entire course of the examination. His digit span was four items forward and three items in reverse. Evaluation of anterograde memory revealed the patient's ability to reproduce four, four and three words on three successive presentations of an eight word supraspan list. He was able to recall none of these words following a brief delay and his recognition memory was unreliable. Remote memory was fair. Evaluation of speech and language revealed dysarthric spontaneous speech that was significant for word finding pauses and dysarthria. There was some difficulty with confrontation naming, but repetition was performed well. There was also some difficulty with comprehension. He was able to write a sentence about the weather, although there were several spelling errors. He was able to read single words. Evaluation of visual functioning revealed considerable difficulty copying a complex geometric design because of spatial displacements, poor organization and omissions. There was difficulty appreciating spatial relationships on a task assessing line orientation. There was no evidence for lateralized neglect. Evaluation of executive functioning revealed a limited mental search strategy. The patient had difficulty on measures of mental control. He was slow and inaccurate.

Cranial nerve evaluation revealed the patient's visual fields to be full to gross confrontation testing. The pupils were round and symmetric from 6 mm to 5 mm. Evaluation of ocular motility revealed full excursions. Facial sensation was preserved, but there was some mild left-sided facial weakness. Auditory acuity was apparently intact. The uvula, tongue and shoulders were symmetric. Evaluation of the motor system revealed a left-sided pronator drift, but direct confrontation assessment of strength failed to reveal any focal motor weakness. Deep tendon reflexes were symmetric. There were no abnormal involuntary movements. Evaluation of coordination revealed accurate finger-nose-finger testing. The patient was able to stand unassisted and the stance was stable. The gait was performed normally. Sensory examination was intact, including vibration in the distal lower extremities.

Murray Grossman, M.D. Associate Professor
Department of Neurology
University of Pennsylvania Medical Center
School of Medicine
Hospital of the University of Pennsylvania

The patient's serum studies included a B12 of 659, TSH of 3.44, a sed rate of 1. I had the opportunity to review the patient's CT scan. This demonstrated a question of some small vessel ischemic disease in a periventricular distribution. There was also a question of some medial temporal atrophy.

Mr. Beckwith has memory, executive, visual and language difficulties that have been progressive in nature. Given the patient's diabetes, I could not rule out small vessel ischemic disease. I suggested an MRI scan of the brain to evaluate the patient for small vessel ischemic disease. Another potential contributing factor could be the patient's hepatitis C and abnormal liver functioning. Of course, there are other metabolic and infectious etiologies that must be ruled out as well and I suggested several serum studies. I also suggested a SPECT scan to evaluate the risk for Alzheimer's Disease. It may be necessary in the future to obtain an EEG and to perform a lumbar puncture, depending on the results of these studies.

Thank you very much for allowing me to participate in the care of this lovely gentleman. Please do not hesitate to call if you have any additional questions.

Sincerely yours,

Murray Grossman, M.D.

MG/05
HN_MG_05.308

cc:
Dr. Bonnie Gardner
301 East City Line Avenue
Bala Cynwyd, PA 19004

Larry Finkelstein, D.O.
4190 City Avenue, Suite 315
Philadelphia, PA 19131

Contacting Jay's Job

Contacting Jay's job, I was a little apprehensive because Jay was out on sick leave for 3½ weeks. Jay had the time because he rarely called out sick. His job was very accommodating, and he has been on the job for over 30 years in various positions. The company loved his performance. I continued to explain that Jay is going out on disability and the medical problems he is experiencing. Jay's supervisor also notices a change, confusion with his performance. He was in that position as a forklift operator for ten years, and with the company for a total of 30 years. His supervisor continued to explain. "He was misplacing products in the areas that they did not belong. The products that he stored with the forklift were not aligned properly in the storage area. The large boxes would fall 3-4 feet to the ground that he had put in place. John had forgotten all that he used to do for the last ten years. He used to train the new employees and continued to mentor them until his illness started to show." At that point in the conversation with Jay's supervisor, I explained to him that Jay was diagnosed with Middle Stage Alzheimer's

I apologize to Jay's supervisor for not keeping the company informed. However, I was so busy with my work schedule, maintaining the household, the children's needs, and staying on top of Jay's Medical conditions. I didn't realize that he could be having problems on the job at the same time the problems started at home.

CHAPTER 5

What Did His Diagnosis Mean For Our Future? What's meant By The Middle Stages Of Alzheimer's Disease?

Long-Term Care Insurance

I was ultimately in denial of my husband's diagnosis. I remember that President Ronald Reagan had this disease. Unfortunately, I still was in the dark about the condition. So I immediately started researching for answers to get a better understanding to find ways to help him. Dr. Grossman's statement, "Mrs. Beckwith, "get your finances in order," haunted me. I honestly thought our finances were sufficient. However, something bothers me about that statement, and I didn't take the time to ask him his reason for that statement. I later learned that I did not have Long Term Care Insurance (LTC)[4]. It conceivably would have helped me much. Nevertheless, it was too late for my husband.

On Tuesday, July 23, 2019, I interviewed Mr. Edgar Parker, Group Leader for the Alzheimer's Caregiver's Support Group at the Anne Arundel Medical Center in Annapolis, Maryland. Mr. Parker was the caregiver of his wife, Jean. He stated in one section of his interview on their jobs at age 55 years old, he and his wife Jean had applied for Long Term Care Insurance(LTC).

---

[4] **Long Term Care (LTC) Insurance. Extended health insurance that exceeds your regular insurance. Covers extended care.**

However, Jean Parker was denied insurance after the insurance doctor's examination findings that Jean had early signs of Alzheimer's Disease. Mr. Parker stated that fortunately, his wife had enough investments of her own to pay for her care. Two days a week, four hours a day, a nurse came into their home to help with her care. And as Alzheimer's diagnosis progress, her investments were used to put her in a long-term care facility.

On Monday, July 29, 2019, I interviewed Mrs. Florence Nightingale (not her real identity, requested to keep her real identity private). I met Florence at one of the Alzheimer's Caregivers Support Groups in Maryland. Florence was the Caregiver of her husband. She states, "those insurance companies need to put up or shut-up." "Because Alzheimer's can be long-term care, the insurance companies don't consider it an illness as such. Unless you have specific Long term Care Insurance (LTC)." An insurance agent was at an Alzheimer's Caregivers Support Group meeting; he said, "I hope you have long-term insurance." Florence told him, "I have another really good insurance." Florence and I had the same understanding of insurance. We had Great health insurance until you or your loved one were diagnosed with Alzheimer's Disease. Florence and her husband also have a home in the North-eastern part of Europe, where she paid health insurance for 21 years. She doesn't want to drop the insurance just in case she goes back there to live. Florence and her husband now would still pay the insurance there and here in the United States. So it was shocking to Florence they did not have Long Term Care Insurance.

In my journey, I reached out to social services agencies, the Department Of Aging, the Department of Welfare, and the Department of Health Services. The feedback I received at that time was there was nothing in place for his age at the moment. I decided to go to Group Support for aging, ages ranging from the late '60s to the '90s. I asked my father to accompany me to The Group Support for aging. So I would not feel out of place, Jay could not attend. He would not be able to sit for that long period because the support group sessions were 90-minute sessions. I realized, at the time, there was not an immediate answer for me. There were individuals of my parents' age. The discussions were about their living arrangements, estate planning, and medicare help. Dementia or

Alzheimer's were not discussed. I felt so out of place, wondering where I should get help. I contacted the Alzheimer's Association about the Walking for a Cure. Jay and I participated in the Walk in Fairmount Park in Philadelphia, Pennsylvania, in 2002. An associate physician recommended me to read the "36 Hour Day" to help me understand the disease, and your day caring for your loved one will be 36 hours. I kept researching and found another book, "Ice Cream In The Cupboard." I had even found the author's phone number and spoke to him about his care for his wife. I still remembered the frustration in his voice. He explained a little more about his ups and downs for caring for his wife. The book was titled because she placed ice cream in their kitchen cabinetry instead of the refrigerator freezer. Ice cream was one of his wife's favorite foods.

I found from The Alzheimer's Association some information on Adult Daycare in the areas of our home, and I visited a few. The places would not have met Jay's needs, in my opinion. No stimulation whatsoever; Adults just sitting around staring into space or looking at each other. At different times of the day, I sometimes revisited the same daycare, hoping I would notice a positive difference. Unfortunately, I did not. I left those facilities depressed. Feeling sorry for the people who were placed there and asking myself, Why? Those people are human beings, not objects just sitting there while the staff just watch TV, or just sitting around holding conversations with each other irrelevant to their jobs. I wanted a facility that gives more stimulation to their patients.

Financial Assistance and Support Services For
People with Disabilities

Today you can explore a wide range of programs and tools to help with housing, taxes, medical bills, service and emotional support animals, and more.

Medicaid For Adults
What help is available?

You may qualify for Medicaid, a joint federal and state program that helps with medical costs for some people with limited income from the Center for Medicare and Medicaid Services (CMS).

Am I eligible?

Each state has different rules about eligibility and applying for Medicaid for adults.

How do I apply?

Each state has different application requirements for Medicaid for adults. Call your state Medicaid program to see if you qualify and to learn how to apply.[5]

Help and Support for Caregivers

These resources and suggestions can help you find emotional and task support as a caregiver for a parent, spouse, or child with special needs.

Federal Government Caregiver Resources

Alzheimer's Caregiving

Learn how to respond to changes in communication and behavior, provide everyday care, and get help when needed.

- Behavior changes and communication in Alzheimer's
  Communication and Behavior Problems:
  Resources for Alzheimer's Caregivers
  *Communicating with a Confused Patient
  *Coping with Agitation or Aggression
  *Safety Concerns
  * Wandering and Alzheimer's Disease

---

[5] The USA.gov

* When a Person with Alzheimer's Rummages and Hides Things
* Alzheimer's and Hallucination, Delusions, and Paranoia
* Tips for Coping with Sundowning
*Big changes in how they act in late afternoon or evening
* Managing Personality and Behavior Changes in Alzheimer's
* Alzheimer's Caregiving: Changes in Communication skills[6]

Preparedness For Alzheimer's Caregivers
In Catastrophic Times

It is important for caregivers to have a disaster plan for the special needs of people with Alzheimer's/Dementia, whose impairments in memory and reasoning severely limit their ability crises. The crises could be weather, fires, floods, earthquakes, and other emergency situations.

In general, you should prepare to meet the needs of your loved one or patient for at least 7 days to be on the safe side of a disaster, including having options if you lose basic services, water, and other essentials to run your home properly. Organizations like the Alzheimer's Associations (ALZ.org) in your area, Alzheimer's Disease International (ADI), Federal Emergency Management Agency (FEMA), International Red Cross, American Red Cross provide information about making a general disaster preparedness plan. The Administration for Community Living has a disaster planning toolkit for people with dementia.

Preparing For A Disaster
A Person With Alzheimer/Dementia

Your kit might contain:

   *Physician's name, address, and phone number
   *Incontinence undergarments, wipes, and lotions
   *Favorite snacks and high-nutrient drinks
   *Pillow, toys or something the person loves that is highly identifiable
   *Copies of legal, medical, insurance, and Social Security information

---

[6] USA.gov

*Recent photos of the person
*Waterproof bags or containers to hold medications and documents

Be sure to place all supplies in a watertight container.

Other supplies you may need are:

*Warm clothing and sturdy shoes
*Spare eyeglasses and hearing-aids batteries
*Medications
*Flashlights and extra batteries

If You Must Leave Home

In some circumstances, you may decide to "ride out" a natural disaster at home. In others, you may need to move to a safer place, like a community shelter or someone's home. Relocation may make the person with Alzheimer's very anxious. Be sensitive to his or her emotions. Stay close, offer your hand, or give the person reassuring hugs.

To plan for an Evacuation
    *Know how to get to the nearest emergency shelters.
    *If you don't drive or driving is dangerous. Arrange transportation help
    *Make sure the person with Alzheimer's is WEARING some source of ID.
    *Take both general supplies and your Alzheimer's emergency kit.

    *Pack familiar, comforting items. If possible, the household pet.
    *Save emergency phone numbers in your communication device.
    *Plan to keep neighbors, friends, and family informed about your location.
    *If conditions are noisy or chaotic, try to find a peaceful area/place.

If You Are Separated

It's very important to stay with a person with Alzheimer's in a disaster. Do not count on the person to stay in one place while you go to get help.

However, the unexpected can happen, so it is a good idea to plan for possible separation:

*Enroll the person for MedicAlert Alzheimer's Association 24/7

Wandering Support Program, is an identification and support program for people who may become lost.

*Prepare for wandering. Place labels in garments to aid in identification.

Keep an article of clothes in a plastic bag to help trained dogs to find him or her.

*Identify specific neighbors or nearby family and friends who would be willing to help in a crisis.

Make plans of action with them should the person with Alzheimer's be unattended during a crisis.

Tell neighbors about the person's specific disabilities, including the inability to follow complex instructions, memory loss, impaired judgment, disorientation, and confusion.

Give examples of simple one-step instruction that the person may be able to follow.

*Give someone you trust a house key and a list of emergency phone numbers.
*Provide local police and emergency service with photos of the person with Alzheimer's and copies of his or her medical documents, so they are aware of the person's needs.

For More Information About Disaster Preparedness
and Alzheimer's

NIA Alzheimer's and related Dementias Education and Referral (ADEAR) dear@nia.hih.gov www.nia.nih.gov/alzheimers

The National Institute on Aging's ADEAR Center offers information and free print publications about Alzheimer's disease and related dementias for families, caregivers, and health professionals. ADEAR Center staff answer telephone, email, written requests and make referrals to local and national resources.

Family Caregiver Alliance
1-800-445-8106 (toll-free)
info@caregiver.org
www.caregiver.org

Eldercare Locator
1-800-677-1116 (toll-free)
eldercare locator@n4a.org
https://eldercare.acl.gov

ECONOMIC VALUE

**The value of services provided by informal caregivers has steadily increased over the last decade with an estimated economic value of $470 billion in 2013, up from $450 billion in 2009 and $375 billion in 2007. [AARP Public Policy Institute. (2015) A Valuing the Invaluable: 2015 Update.]

**At $470 billion in 2013, the value of paid home care total Medicaid spending in the same year, and nearly matched the value of the sales of the world's largest company, WALMART ($477 billion). AARP Public Policy Institute. (2015). Valuing the Invaluable: 2015 Update.

**The economic value of the care provided by unpaid caregivers of those with Alzheimer's disease or other dementias was $217.7 billion in 2014. [Alzheimer's Association (2015). 2015 Alzheimer's Disease Facts and Figures.]

Self-Directed Services

I am familiar with this service personally because my sister uses this service. It means participants, or their representatives, If applicable, have decision-making authority over certain services and take direct responsibility to manage their services with the assistance of a system of available supports—the self-directed service, such as an agency delivery model. Self-direction of services allows participants to have the responsibility for managing all aspects of service delivery in a person-centered planning process.

Self-direction promotes personal choices and control over the delivery of waiver and state plan services, including who provides the services and how services are provided. For example, participants afforded the decision-making authority to recruit, hire, train, supervise the individuals who furnish their services. The Centers for Medicare & Medicaid Services (CMS) calls this "employer authority." CMs refers to this as "budget authority."[7]

This type of service is workable, in my opinion, if you are great at managing your finances and supervise others with ease while staying healthy.

---

[7] Medicaid.gov

Who Are Family Caregivers?

Based on the American Psychological Association, and the National Alliance for Caring, as of January 2001, 65.7 million Americans(or 29 percent of the U.S adult population involving 31 percent of all U.S. households) served as family caregivers for an ill or disabled relative. In 2015-2016, Behavioral Risk Factor Surveillance System (BRFSS) Data from Adults in 38 States, Puerto Rico, and the District of Columbia 1 in 5 adults were caregivers. Caregivers provide regular care or assistance to Friends or Family members with a health problem or disability.

About 43.2 million Americans provide unpaid care to an adult in the last 12 months. {National Alliance for Caregiving AARP.(2015). Caregiving the U.S.} Most Caregivers, 85%, care for one another adult, while 15% care for two adults. {National Alliance for Caregiving and AARP. (2015), Caregiving, and AARP. (2015), Caregiving in the {US}.

Approximately 39.8 million caregivers provide care to adults (aged 18+) with a disability or illness or 16% of Americans. {Coughlin, J.(2010). Estimating the Impact of Caregiving and Employment on Well-Being: Outcomes & Insight Health Management.
About 15.7 million adult family caregivers care for someone who has Alzheimer's disease or other dementia.[Alzheimer's Association. {2010}.2015 Alzheimer's Disease Facts and Figures.] Nearly 10% provide care to someone with dementia. Lengthy Half have provided care for at least two years. Intense 30% have provided at least 20 hours per week.

Future Caregivers, 1 in 6 Non-Caregivers, expect to become Caregivers within two years according to CDC.gov/aging August 2018 Center for Disease Control. 37% are caring for a parent or parent-in-law, 20% are 65 years old or older. Over half assist with personal care, 4 in 5 manage household tasks.

VETERAN: *There are a total of 5.5 million caregivers caring for former or current Military
Personnel in the U.S (1.1 million posts 9/11). [Ramchand, R; Tanielian T; Fisher, M; Vaughan, C; Trail; Batka, C; Voorhies, P; Robbins, M; Robinson, E; & Ghosh-Dastidar B. (2014). Key Facts and Statistics from

the RAND Military Caregivers Study.]* 9 in 10 (96%) caregivers of veterans are female, and 70% provide care to their spouse or partner. 30% of veterans' caregivers nationally, 88% report increased stress or anxiety as a result of caregiving, and 77% state sleep deprivation as an issue. [National Alliance for Caregiving and United Health Foundation. (2010). Caregivers of Veterans: Serving on the Home Front.] Military caregivers after 9/11 are more likely to be employed (63% vs. 47%), younger (37% under 30 years old vs. 11%), more likely to be caring for a recipient with a behavioral health condition (64% vs.36%). Or VA disability rating (58% vs. 30%). [Ramchand R; Tanielian, T; Fisher, M; Vaughan, C; Trail, T; Batka C; Voorhies P; Robbins, M; Robinson E; & Ghosh-Dastidar, B.(2014). Key Facts and Statistics from RAND Military Caregivers Study.] Veterans suffer more frequently from traumatic Brain Injury(29%), Post-traumatic Stress Disorder, Diabetes (28%), and paralysis or Spinal Cord Injury (20%). [National Alliance for Caregiving and United Health Foundation. (2010). Caregivers of Veterans: Serving on the Home Front.]

GENDER: *65% of care recipients are female, with an average age of 69.4. The younger the care recipient, the more likely the recipient to be male. 45% of recipients aged 18-45 are males, while 33% of recipients aged 50 or higher are male{National Alliance for Caregiving in the U.S.] *Upward of 75% of all Caregivers are females, and may spend as much as 50% more time providing care than males.{Institute Of Aging.(2016). Read How IOA Views in American] *Male caregivers are less likely to provide personal care, but 24% help a loved one get dressed compared to 28% of female caregivers. 16% of males help with bathing versus 30% of females. 40% of males caregivers use paid assistance for a loved one's personal care. About 14.5 million caregivers are males out of the 43.4% who care for an older family member. [National Alliance for Caregiving and AARP. (2009) Caregiving in the U.S.]

CARING IN THE LESBIAN, GAY, BISEXUAL, & TRANSEXUAL (LGBT) COMMUNITIES.
*9% of caregivers self-identify as LBGT. [National Alliance for Caregiving and AARP. (2015). Caregiving in the U.S.*there are at least 3 million LGBT people aged 55+ in the U.S. This number is expected to double in the next two decades, [Espinoza, R. (2014) Out and Visible: The Experiences and Attitudes of Lesbian, Gay, Bisexual, and Transgender Older Adults, Ages 45-75]

*Male caregivers report providing more hours of care than female caregivers. The average weekly hours of care provided by females from both LGBT and general population samples is similar-26 vs. 28 hours-but LGBT males from the comparison sample (41 hours vs. 29). It reflects that are full-time caregivers, spending over 150 hours per week in this capacity, compared to 3% of Lesbian 2%, Bisexual respondents.[MetLife. (2010) Still Out, Still Aging: Study of Lesbian, Gay, Bisexual, and Transgender Baby Boomers]

*LGBT Individuals are most likely to be very concerned about having enough money 51% vs. 36%, experiencing loneliness in old age (32% vs. 19%), declining physical health (43% vs. 33%) or not having to take care of themselves (43% vs. 34%) or not having anybody to take of them (30% vs.16%) compared to non-LGBT. [Fredriksen-Goldsen, K.l; Kim H. J; Emlet, C. A; Muraco, A; Erosheva, E. A; Hoy-Ellis, C. P; Goldsen, J; & Petry, H.(2011). The Aging and Health Report: Disparities and Resilience among Lesbian, Gay, Bisexual, and Transgender Older Adults.]

*20% of older LGBT individuals feel their relationship with their healthcare provider would be adversely affected if their health provider would know their sexual orientation/gender. [Fredriksen-Golden, K. l; Kim, H-J; Emlet, C. A; Muraco, A; Erosheva, E. A; Hoy-Ellis, C. P; Goldensen, J R; Petry, H.(2011). The Aging and Health Report: Disparities and Resilience among Lesbian, Gay, Bisexual, and Transgender Older Adults.] *LGBT older adults are twice as age as a single person to reside alone, and three to four times less likely to have children.[MetLife. (2010. Still Aging: The MetLife Study of Lesbian, Gay, Bisexual, Transgender Baby Boomers.]

OLDER ADULTS WITH DEVELOPMENTAL DISABILITIES*There are an estimated 641,000 adults aged 60+with cognitive and other Disabilities (e.g., cerebral, autism, epilepsy, traumatic brain injury). **This number is projected to double to 1,242,794 by 2030, coinciding with the aging population of baby boomers born between 1946 and 1964. [Heller, T. (2011). Strength for Caring: Older Adults with Developmental Disabilities and Their Aging Family Caregivers.] Families are still the primary caregivers for adults with developmental disabilities and are themselves aging. About 76% of individuals with developmental disabilities reside at home.

In 25% of these homes, the family caregiver is 60 years of age. The average age of the care recipient with a developmental disability is age 38. [Heller, T.*(2011).Strength for Caring: Older Adults with Developmental Disabilities and Their Aging Family Caregiver.

NIH〉National Institute on Aging

CAUSES OF ALZHEIMER'S DISEASE

Alzheimer's Disease in People with Down Syndrome

Many, but not all, people with Down syndrome develop Alzheimer's disease when they get older.

People with Down syndrome are born with an extra copy of chromosome 21, which carries the APP gene. This gene produces a specific protein called amyloid precursor protein (APP). Too much APP protein leads to a buildup of protein clumps called beta-amyloid plaques in the brain. By age 40, almost all people with Down syndrome have these plaques, along with other protein deposits, called tau tangles, which cause problems with how brain cells function and increase the risk of developing Alzheimer's dementia.

However, not all people with these brain plaques will develop the symptoms of Alzheimer's. Estimates suggest that 50 percent or more of people with Down syndrome will develop dementia due to Alzheimer's disease as they age. People with Down syndrome begin to show symptoms of Alzheimer's disease in their 50s or 60s.

This type of Alzheimer's is not passed down from a parent to a child.

Down Syndrome and Alzheimer's Research

Scientists are working hard to understand why some people with Down syndrome develop dementia while others do not. They want to know how Alzheimer's disease begins and progresses, so they can develop drugs or other treatments that can stop, delay, or even prevent the disease process.

Research in this area includes:

- Basic studies to improve our understanding of the genetic and biological causes of brain abnormalities that lead to Alzheimer's
- Observational research to measure cognitive changes in people over time
- Studies of biomarkers (biological signs of disease), brain scans, and other tests that may help diagnose Alzheimer's—even before symptoms appear—and show brain changes as people with Down syndrome age
- Clinical trials to test treatments for dementia in adults with Down syndrome

Learn about Alzheimer's Disease Research Opportunities

- Join DS-Connect®, a voluntary, confidential, online registry from the Eunice Kennedy Shriver National Institute of Child Health and Human Development (part of the National Institutes of Health, or NIH). You, your legally authorized representative, or your guardian can submit information about your health and choose to be contacted about research opportunities, if desired. Email DS-Connect® for more information and to sign up.
- Learn more about the Alzheimer's Biomarkers Consortium of Down Syndrome (ABC-DS) and how to participate
- Learn about the Alzheimer's Clinical Trials Consortium - Down Syndrome

https://www.nia.nih.gov/health/alzheimers-disease-people-down-syndrome#:~:text=Estimates suggest that 50 percent,a parent to a child

7/29/2020   Alzheimer's Disease in People with Down Syndrome | National Institute on Aging

- Search the National Institute on Aging's Alzheimer's disease Clinical Trials Finder.
- Look at the National Down Syndrome Society's directory of studies .

For More Information About Down Syndrome and Alzheimer's

Down Syndrome and Alzheimer's Disease Resources

- Alzheimer's Disease and Down Syndrome (National Down Syndrome Society)
- Down Syndrome and Alzheimer's Disease   (Alzheimer's Association)
- Aging and Down Syndrome: A Health & Well-Being Guidebook (PDF, 8.0M) (National Down Syndrome Society)

Down Syndrome Research and Resources

- Down Syndrome Consortium
- Down Syndrome: Overview (National Institute of Child Health and Human Development)
- DS-Connect® The Down Syndrome Registry

This content is provided by the National Institute on Aging (NIA), part of the National Institutes of Health. NIA scientists and other experts review this content to ensure that it is accurate, authoritative, and up to date.

Content reviewed: May 19, 2017

RELATIONSHIPS BETWEEN CAREGIVERS
AND CARE RECIPIENTS

*A vast majority of caregivers (85%) care for a relative or other love one:**42% care for a parent (31% for a mother, 11% for a father); **15% care for a friend, neighbor, or another non-relative; **14% care for a child; **7% care for a parent-in-law; **7 care for a grandparent or grandparent-in law. [National Alliance for Caregiving and AARP (2015) Caregiving in the U.S.] Parent care continues to be the primary caregiving.

Situation for mid-life caregivers, with 70% of the caregivers between the ages of 50 and 64. [Wagner, D. & Takagi, E. (2010). Health Affairs: Informal Caregiving by and for Older Adults.] *Most care recipients reside in their own homes (48%), and one in three (35%) reside in their caregiver's home. 3 in 10 care recipients who are not in assisted living or skilled nursing facilities reside alone (31%). [National Alliance for Caregiving AARP. (2009 & 2015) U.S.]

Race and Ethnicity

Individual adult caregivers in the U.S. identify their race/ethnicity as the following:

White: 62%
African-American 13%
Hispanic (non-White, non-African-American) 17%
Asian-American 6%
[National Alliance for Caregiving and AARP (2015) Caregiving in the U.S] Hispanic (non-White, non-African-American) caregivers have the highest reported prevalence among other racial/ethnic groups are as follows:
African- American: 20.3%
Asian 19.7%
White 16.9%
[National Alliance for Caregiving and AARP(2015) Caregiving in the U.S.]

On average, white caregivers are older(52.5 years old than their counterparts among other races/ethnicities. The average of caregivers among different racial/ethnic groups is Asian-American 46.6 years old **African-American 44.2% years old** Hispanic(non-White, non-African-American: 42.7 years old [National Alliance for Caregiving and AARP. (2015). Personal care attendance [in the U.S.] *Hispanic (non-White, non-African-American) and African-American caregivers experience burden from caregiving and spend more time caregiving on average than their white or Asian peers. The percentage of high burden caregivers caregiving time by racial/ethnic groups is **African-American: 57%, 30 hours per week **White 33%, 20 hours per week.

**Asian-American: 30%, 20 hours per week to 16 hours per week [Alzheimer's Association. (2015). Alzheimer's Disease Facts and Figures.] *More than half of African-American caregivers find themselves "sandwiched" between caring for an older person and a younger person under the age of 18. After more than one more senior person.

African-American caregivers are also more likely to reside with the care recipient and spend 20.6 hours per week providing care. Also, 66 percent of African-Americans caregivers employed full or part-time. [National Alliance for Caregiving and AARP. (2015). Caregiving in the U.S.]
*The needs of care recipients vary by race/ethnicity. African-American caregivers (41%) are more likely to provide help with more than three ADLs than whites caregivers (28%) or Asian-Americans (23%). [Alzheimer's Association. (2015) 2015 Alzheimer's Disease Facts and Figures.]

TIME SPENT *CAREGIVING*

*4 in 10 (40%) caregivers are in high-burden situations, 18% medium burden, and 41% low burden based on the Level of Care Index (1997). The weight of care increased with hours of care provided; 92% of providers offering 21 or more hours per week are high burden versus 16% of lower hour providers—[National Alliance for Caregiving and AARP.(2015). Caregiving in the U.S] .*Primary family caregivers of people with dementia report spending an average of 9 hours per day providing help to relatives. [Fisher, G. G; Franks, M. M; Plassman, B. L; Brown, S.L; Potter G. G; Llewellyn, D; et al. (2011). Caring for Individuals with Dementia and Cognitive Impairment, not Dementia: Findings from the Aging, Demographics, and Memory Study.]

HOURS PER WEEK

Family caregivers spend an average of 24.4 hours per week, providing care. Nearly 1 in 4 caregivers spend 41 hours or more per week providing care [National Alliance for Caregiving and AARP. (2015). Caregiving in the U.S.] *Family caregivers who reside with those they provide care for spend 40.5 hours per week caring for this person.**Those caring for a spouse/partner spend 44.6 hours per week performing caregiving tasks. **Those caring for a child under 18 spend 29.7 hours per week performing caregiving tasks—[National Alliance for Caregiving and AARP.(2015). Caregiving in the U.S. and other parts of the world *Older caregivers who are 75+ years old provide 34 hours in an average week on caregiving. Middle-aged caregivers report spending 21.7 hours per week on caregiving tasks. [National Alliance for Caregiving and AARP. (2015). 2015 Alzheimer's Disease and other Dementias provide an estimated 21.9 hours of care per week. [Alzheimer's Association. (2015) Alzheimer's Disease Facts and Figures]

MONTHS AND YEARS PROVIDING CARE

The average duration of a caregiver's role in four years. **Only 30% of caregivers provide care less than a year. **24% of caregivers provide care for more than five years. **15% of caregivers provide care for ten or more years. Higher-hour caregivers are twice as likely to have been in their caregiving role for ten years or more. [National Alliance for Caregiving and AARP. (2015). Personal care attendants [in the U.S.]* Regardless of employment status, unpaid caregivers report that positive activities in their respective daily lives are reduced by 27.2% due to their caregiving responsibilities. This effect is three times greater in personal lives than in their professional lives. [Coughlin, J. (2010). Estimating the Impact of Caregiving and Employment on Well-Being: Outcomes & Insights in Health Management.] *Measured by the duration of care, Alzheimer's and Dementia caregivers provide care on average 1-4 years more than caregivers caring for someone with an illness other than Alzheimer's Disease. They are also more likely to be providing care for five years or longer. [Alzheimer's Association. (2015). 2015 Alzheimer's Disease Facts and Figures.]

GEOGRAPHIC DISTANCE BETWEEN CAREGIVERS AND RECIPIENT

*The vast majority of caregivers (74%) reside three within 20 minutes of their care recipient. 13% of caregivers reside between 20 minutes and an hour away from their care recipient.**The proportion of caregivers reporting they live fewer than 20 minutes from their care recipient has increased steadily over the past ten years(44% in 2004, 51% in2009, and 75% in 2015).[Alliance for Caregiving and AARP. (2015.) Caregiving in the U.S.]

*As the age of the caregiver's increases, their distance from their recipient decreases. 84% of caregivers aged 75+ reside within 20 minutes of their care recipient, compared to their caregiving peers in other aged brackets50-64. **74% of caregivers aged 18-49 [National Alliance for Caregiving and AARP. (2015). Caregiving in the U.S.] *48% of care recipients reside in their own homes. **Higher-hour care recipients are less likely to live in their homes (28%) than lower-hour recipients (57%).

Inversely, higher-hour care recipients are more likely to live in their caregiver's house (62%) than lower-hour recipients (22%). [National Alliance for Caregiving and AARP. (2015.) Caregiving in the U.S.] *Approximately 5-7 million caregivers in a million caregivers in the U.S. (about 15% of all caregivers) are long-distance caregivers. This number will double by 2020. [National Council on Aging. (2006). Near 7 million Long-Distance Caregivers, Maker Work, and Person Sacrifices.]

Long-distance caregivers have the highest annual expenses (about $8,728) compared to co-resident caregivers ($5,885) or those who care for a loved one nearby (about $4,570). [AARP Public Policy Institute. (2008), Valuing the Invaluable: The Economic Value of Family Caregiving.]
*Long-distance caregivers reside an average of 450 miles (724km) from their care recipients (or approximately 7 hours of travel time).

**More males (58%) than females (42%) are long-distance caregivers. [National Alliance for Caregiving the MetLife Mature Market Institute. (2004). Miles Away: The MetLife Study of Long-Distance Caregiving.]

*Long-distance caregivers are more likely to report emotional distress (47%) than caregivers either residing with their care recipient (43%) or residing less than one hour (28%). [National Alliance for Caregiving and AARP. (2004). Caregiving in the U.S.]

*Caregivers who do not reside with their care receiver live the following distance from those they care: [Gallup-Healthways. (2011). Gallup-Healthways Well-Being Survey: Caregiving Cost U.S. Economy $25.2 Billion in Lost Productivity.]

CAREGIVING IN RURAL AREAS

*More than half of the 65 million Americans living in rural areas are over 50. Elders in rural areas (about a quarter of all elders) are more likely to reside alone, near or at the poverty level, and suffer from a chronic condition or physical disability. They require an average of 46 miles of travel to get the nearest health professional. [U.S. Department of Health and Human Services Rural Task and Human Services Rural Task. (2002). HHS Rural Task Force Report.]

*3.6 million Americans are distant caregivers who provide care for family members that reside 450 miles away. [National Alliance for Caregiving & AARP. (2005). Caregiving in the U.S.]

*About 51% of caregivers in rural areas used community-based services. [Buckwater K. C; & Davis, L.L. (2009) Elder Caregiving in Rural Communities].

CAREGIVING TASK

*On average, caregivers spend **13 days each month on the task such as shopping, food preparation, housekeeping laundry, transportation, giving medication; **6 days per month on feeding, dressing, grooming, walking, bathing, and assistance toileting, **13 hours per month researching care services or information on the disease, coordinating physician visits or managing financial matters [Gallup-Healthways Well-Being Index].

*Of family caregivers who provide complex chronic care: **46% perform medical and nursing tasks; **96% provide help nursing tasks; ** 96% provide help with Activities of Daily Living (ADLs) such as taking prescribed medications, shopping for groceries, transportation, or using technology, or both. [AARP and United Health Hospital Fund. (2012). Home Alone: Family Caregivers Providing Complex Chronic Care.]* On average, caregivers perform 1.7 of 6 ADLs, most commonly getting in and out of beds and chairs (43%). According to the National Alliance for Caregiving and AARP.(2015). Caregiving in the U.S.*On average, caregivers perform 4.2 of 7 ADLs, most commonly transportation (78%), grocery or other shopping (76%), and housework (72%). [National Alliance for Caregiving and AARP.(2015). Caregiving in the U.S.]

*57% Of caregivers report that they do not have a choice about performing clinical tasks and that this lack of choice is deliberate. **43% feel that these tasks are their individual responsibility because no one else can do it or because insurance will not pay for a professional caregiver, **12 reports that they are pressured to perform these tasks by a care receiver. **8% report that they are influenced to perform these tasks by another family member [AARP and United and Health Hospital Fund. (2012). Complex Chronic Care.]

*Caregivers report holding significant decision-making authority regarding the following: **Monitoring of the care recipient's condition and adjusting care(66%);
**Communicating with healthcare professionals on behave of the care recipient (63%); ** Acting as an advocate for the care recipient with care providers, community services, or government agencies (50%). [National Alliance for Caring and AARP. (2015). Caregiving in the U.S.]

ELDER ABUSE

**The Department of Health defines abuse as "a violation of an individual's human and civil rights by another person." Abuse can take many forms, including physical, psychological, sexual, or financial abuse, discrimination, or neglect. *Under this definition, as many as 25% of elder care recipients report significant abuse. [Cooper, C; Selwood, A; & Livingston, G, (2008). The Prevalence of Elder Abuse and Neglect: A Systematic Review]

Approximately 1 out of 10 Americans aged 60+ have experienced some form of elder abuse. Some estimates range as high as 5 million elders who are abused each year. [National Council on Aging. (2016). Elder Abuse Facts]Only 7% of elder abuse cases are ever reported to authorities. [National Research Council. (2003). Elder Mistreatment: Abuse, Neglect, and Exploitation in an Aging America.] ** For every 1 case of elder abuse known to programs and agencies, there are 24 new cases. [Lifespan of Greater Rochester, Inc; Weill Cornell Medical Center of Cornell University & New York City Department for Aging. (2011) Under the Radar: New York State Elder Prevalence Study.]

**Elder abuse, even modest abuse, increases death by 300% compared to elders who exploit. Dong, X; Simon, M. A; Beck, T; Farran, C; McCann, J; Mendes deLeon, C; et al. (2011). Elder abuse and the direct medical costs associated with violent injuries to older adults are estimated to add over $5.3 billion. The nation's annual health expenditures and the annual financial loss by victims of elder commercial exploitation expected to be $2.9 billion in 2009, a 12% increase from 2008. [Administration Aging: National Center on Elder Abuse. (2016).Statistics/Data: Impact of Elder Abuse].

The United States Senate Passes Bill To Protect Seniors with Alzheimer's And Other Dementias From Elder Abuse

Washington-Approximately one in 10 seniors age 60 and older have experienced some form of elder abuse. For people with Alzheimer's and related dementias, some estimates are putting it at just over 50 percent.

August 2020, The U.S. Senate unanimously passed legislation authored by Senators Susan Collins, Bob Menendez, and Chuck Grassley to protect seniors with dementia from harm and exploitation. The Promoting Alzheimer's Awareness to Prevent Elder Abuse Act would ensure that the

Department of Justice's elder abuse training materials considers individuals with Alzheimer's disease and related dementias.

"America's seniors too often face abuse and exploitation. Preventing and responding to these crimes can be particularly challenging in cases involving Alzheimer's and or other forms of dementia. It is great to lead the recent effort to strengthen the Justice Department's tools to combat elder abuse, and I'm grateful that the Senate passed this important bill to equip law enforcement with critical training to better respond to cases involving Alzheimer's and dementia," Grassley said.

"Chairman of the Senate Aging Committee, one of my top priorities is protecting our seniors against abuse. During a pandemic, there may be an increased risk for elder abuse, including elder financial exploitation. Our bill would help to ensure that the frontline professionals who are leading against elder abuse have the training needed to respond to cases where the victim or witness has Alzheimer's disease or other forms of dementia," said Collins, founder and co-chair of the Congressional Task Force on Alzheimer's Disease.

"I am thrilled that the Senate has unanimously passed our bill, fully recognizing that we must address the fact that as the number of Americans struggling with Alzheimer's disease and dementia continues to grow, so does the potential for exploitation, physical or emotional abuse, and neglect. We must do more to provide the education caregivers, social service, and health providers. Law enforcement and others need to understand the unique symptoms people with AD/ADRD may have, as well as the training necessary to ensure they are safe from abuse and can live with dignity," Menendez said.

The legislation is support by the Alzheimer's Association, Alzheimer's Foundation of America, Alzheimer's Impact Movement, Elder Justice Coalition, American Geriatric Society, American Society on Aging, B'nai B'rith International, Gerontological Society of America, International Association for Indigenous Aging, Jewish Federations of North America, Justice in Aging, LEAD Coalition (Leaders Engaged on Alzheimer's

Disease), National Adult Protective Services Association, National Association of Area Agencies on Aging (N4A), National Association of Elder Law Attorneys, and

SAGE: Advocacy and Services for LGBT Elders.

CHAPTER 6

Try To Maintain Normalcy, For Our Lives, But I can't. His Diagnosis Will Never Ever Let Us Again ... "The Intruder" Alzheimer's

Jay loved working around the house, so I encouraged Jay to start working around the house while I was at work. We made a list of the various things Jay wanted to do and then went out and purchased the tools and paint, etc., needed to address all his interests and what he wanted to do around the house.

I was thrilled to start Jay on a project while I worked. So he started out painting the foyer. Jay had painted various rooms around the house many times before. He was always elegant, careful, and a good painter. I asked my sister, who was off from work that day, if she would mind checking on him since he is at home painting. She was more than happy to help me out. When she arrived, my sister said, Jay, opened the door very confused. He had spilled paint all over the floor, paint splashes all over the walls, and dripping down were chunks of paint rolling down to the floor. I had two lovely paintings hanging in the foyer; they're destroyed. My twin sister called me frantic, "Jeanette, you need to come home as soon as possible. Jay has made a mess. I will stay with him until you get home." My sister opened the door when I arrived. Nervously, I walked into my home, and I was shocked. Jeanette, my sister, said, "Jay's been sad since I've been here."

I said to my husband and rubbed his face at the same time, telling him it was okay. I looked around, and the paint was everywhere. It looked like a 4-year-old had got a gallon of paint playing in the foyer. Regular chores around the house are no longer viable; the dynamics have changed.

The following incident, Jay received a letter in the mail from a local bank. Jay has opened a new 401 retirement account. He was transferring funds to this account without my knowledge. I asked Jay, "when and why are you opening a new retirement account." He replied, "what are you talking about?" I did not open a new bank account. I showed him the letter from the bank. Jay had no memory of the transaction. It did not surprise me.

The next day I went into the bank and sat down with the branch manager. I showed him the letter that Dr. Grossman had sent. I informed the manager that my husband was diagnosed with progressive Alzheimer's Disease, and he had no memory of this transaction. The manager said, "excuse me. I'll be right back." When he returned, he had paperwork with Jay's signature granting this transaction. He apologized with arrogance in his voice. "Mrs. Beckwith, however, your husband came in and signed on his own. The bank will honor this transaction. If he is ill as you say he is, I will need something in writing from the doctor." I told the bank manager I would be back.

The next day, I contacted Dr. Grossman's secretary. I explained what had happened. She said she would get the letter to me as soon as possible with Dr. Grossman's signature. Within two days, I had the letter in my possession. The letter was detailed enough to give anyone who read the letter that Jay was in no condition to make any rational decisions. Let alone a financial one. I immediately took the letter to the branch manager. He read the letter, made a copy of the letter, and transferred the funds back to Jay's account. I thanked him and left.

No Longer Could Perform His Duties At Church

I later learned Jay could no longer perform his duties at church. We continued arriving at church at 10:50 a.m. every Sunday, and Jay sat with the deacon in the deacon's area of the church while I sat with the congregation with my mother. I was close enough to observe Jay. After the Bishop's message to the community, Sunday's offering was the next same time every Sunday. Jay was used to this routine. Jay and two other deacons would bring the offering table to the center of the pulpit. The congregation would walk around and drop their offering in the basket on the offering table. Usually, Jay interacts with the deacons standing there during offering time and gathering the various bills together $5, $10, $20, etc.

This particular Sunday, I noticed the unusual expression on Jay's face. It reminded me of the time when he had made a mess in the foyer at home painting. This blank stare on his face and not moving. I labeled this look "The Alz Stare," meaning "the stare of memory loss and fixated eyes" I was sitting beside my mother. She asked me, "is Jay alright?" I immediately said yes; knowingly, the real answer was no. When I first informed my parents of Jay's diagnosis, I asked them to please keep his illness private. My family didn't understand why I wanted to stay private. The reasons were I had to understand this diagnosis for myself. Explaining his condition to his peers was not an option for me at the time. At times his condition looked more psychological.

I recall this minister at our church would directly harass Jay. Jay's responsibilities as a deacon were slowly deteriorating. This particular minister secretly made requests to "do this; do that." Every Sunday, when we returned home from church, this was our discussion, "this minister." I realized that Jay's stamina as a man was also deteriorating.

I wanted to approach this minister myself to tell him back the HELL off my husband. But, it would have opened up a whole new negative situation that I didn't have time to battle with the minister and the church services.

Later my siblings noticed a difference in Jay. I asked my sisters to please keep his diagnosis private. My family spoke to me about Jay's condition. They asked me to stop pretending everything was great. Jay is not well; something is wrong, and others are noticing the changes in Jay's behavior. Eventually, Jay was no longer able to attend church.

My Limousine Business Was Affected

Jay worked for the Limo Business that I started, he was a chauffeur. He drove the 1947 Packard Clipper. At the time, Jay was the only driver for that vehicle because it's a three-gear shift. He was teaching my nephew and me how to operate the three-gear shift. I also had a ten-passenger Limo which my nephew and I only operated.

The limo business continued to get booking for the Packer Clipper. Customers loved the Packer for their wedding. Still, Jay was the main driver, not thinking Alzheimer's would affect his driving. But I was mistaken. I had a wedding booked, and Jay drove the Packer while my nephew rode with him to help out if needed. I was out that day with friends at a fashion show and lunch. My nephew called me while I was ordering my lunch. "He said the wedding went well. However, when they drove the couple to the site to take pictures, Jay had forgotten how to start the Packer. The Bride and Groom were so upset that they asked friends to drive them to their reception."

Immediately, I apologized to my friends and told them I had an emergency, and left the restaurant. I drove frantically to the site where the couple was taking their pictures. The couple had left. After five minutes of my arrival, I had started the Packer, and my nephew drove the Packer home. I then proceeded to go to the reception hall to meet with the couple. When I arrived, I spoke to the bride's mother and told her I would refund her money and give them a free dinner for two. I asked her to please accept my apologies. The bride's mother briefly spoke to her daughter. The bride and her mother both accepted—their refund and dinner tickets they received within a week.

When I arrived back home from speaking to the bride's mother, Jay was in the bedroom, resting. I realized there were signs before the wedding that Jay's memory was deteriorating. Not remembering what type of fuel the Packer used and always misplacing the keys to the Packer and his Ford Explorer. After the wedding incident, I was determined to learn how to drive the 1947 Packer Clipper. Fortunately, my son, nephew, and son-in-law learned how to operate the business, transporting customers to their desired destination safely.

On a nice sunny day, Jay and I went out on this vacant parking lot near the house. We exchanged seats, and Jay began to instruct me on how to drive the three gears smoothly. Everything was going well, and we had decided to exchange seats again for him to ride further out for about five to ten miles. On the way back home, we heard a horn blowing on the driver's side. I looked at the other driver and happened to notice the confused look on Jay's face. I asked, "are you alright?" All of a sudden, Jay continued driving through the stop sign. "You just drove through the stop sign," I said to him. He continues to be incoherent, keeps driving. There is a red light ahead; he never slows down. He went right through the red light! I started screaming, "you just drove through the red light, please pullover. Did you see the stop sign a few blocks back?" He replied, "I'm fine." He continued driving." He never responded to me about the stop sign or red light. I prayed all the way home, thanking God traffic was light, and we did not get into an accident. The moment he pulled into the driveway. I decided that would be the last time he drives. I secretly took all the keys to the cars and hid them. Ironically, he never asks for them. The neurologist at the beginning of his diagnosis warned me. Driving will be too difficult. He will have to stop driving. Well, that time is here.

Continually Trying To Stay Grounded With Our Usual Social Life No Longer Existed That Scenario Too

Visiting friends out of state, we would always stay at their home. This particular visit was challenging. Our friends knew Jay was diagnosed with Alzheimer's Disease. However, our friendship did not change. It was early afternoon when Jay and I arrived at Andy and Reginald's home. The four of us decided to go to their pool area. Andy and I sat under an umbrella sipping ice tea, talking, and laughing. Jay and Reginald started swimming in their pool. About five minutes later, Reginald climbed out of the water to get something out of the house. Immediately, I looked over at Jay. He had swum over to the deep side of the pool and was struggling to stay afloat. Reginald was back in the pool, helping Jay swim over to the pool's

31/2 feet side. Jay had forgotten how to swim. Jay was a good swimmer. I ran over to the poolside, and he was okay. We just stayed on the 31/2 feet side with our feet in the water.

That evening after dinner, watching TV, and a great conversation, we all decided to call it a night. Our room was in their basement, and Jay's favorite, a pool table. As we were walking down the stairs, I said to my husband, "let's play a couple of pool games before we go to bed." I walked into the other room where the pool table was, turned around, and Jay was not there. He was in the other room at the bottom of the stairs. I said, "come Jay, let's play a game of pool." He replied, "I don't want to play pool. I don't like the pool." "What!" I said. "You love playing pool," I said to him. "That's why you purchase the pool table for our home." Then I realized Jay stopped going to our basement to play. The last time he played, we played together. I was not that good at playing pool. He was teaching me. But that particular time, I outscored him for the first time. I realized he has FORGOTTEN HOW TO PLAY POOL. My eyes were getting full of tears. I turned my head so he would not notice. We both were tired, so we went straight to bed.

Later that night, Jay wanders up the basement stairs trying to go out of their front door. Their house alarm went off, and I immediately woke up. Jay was not in bed or anywhere in the basement. I ran upstairs, and Reginald nervously ran down his stairs. We both found Jay in the foyer in the dark, just standing there with this blank stare on his face. [The Alz. Stare"] I said, "Jay, what are you doing? You can't go outside at night?" The sound of the alarm seems to make him more disoriented. My friend's husband hurried to disarm the house alarm.

I apologized over and over again to our friends. They were very understanding. My husband and I returned to the basement. I spoke to him in a very soft tone, "Jay, you can't walk around their home; you will trigger their alarm." He just replied, "I'm sorry." I replied, Okay, it's fine; just try to go back to sleep." Jay laid down and eventually went back to sleep. I, on the other hand, could not go back to sleep or relax. I just stay awake for the rest of the night.

In the interview that I conducted with other caregivers, one of the crucial concerns is Wandering. Mr. Parker had experience wandering with his wife. Mr. Parker stated that the first time. "I knew where she was. The police would advise me always to know what she is wearing." The second time Jean wandered away, I couldn't find her. I called the police. They realized I volunteered there. (The law takes good care of their volunteers) so they called the Chief of Police near where I live. (I used to volunteer at my neighborhood police station). When the chief arrived, we were talking, and suddenly we heard the water running. The police chief and I went upstairs, looking around. We found Jean in one of our walk-in closets hiding. She had crawled under the rugs in the back of the closet, so no one could see her.

"Another time she wandered in the garage in the winter, and it was cold. I had to call someone that handles cases with that type of situation so they could get her to come into the house. Eventually, she came in on her own."

Family Vacation

It's time for a family vacation, so I booked a five-day cruise to Cancun, Mexico. Jay, my daughter, son, and I were all excited. We started packing. I decided to call Jay's neurologist to ask if I should do anything particularly special for Jay while we were cruising. Dr. Grossman replied, "I don't think he's going to do well on a cruise Mrs. Beckwith. He could become very agitated because of the new environment." I assured Dr. Grossman we would stay close to him. "My children and I will not let him out of our eyesight." Dr. Grossman said, "This is your decision, Mrs. Beckwith." I thanked him and hung up the phone. Jay loves traveling. I just knew it would help him. But I was wrong. He was no longer interested. It was a disaster, and this is what happened.

The cruise vacation was here! My nephew drove us to the Philadelphia International Airport in our business Limousine. We boarded our flight and flew to Florida, then boarded the ship, and everything was going so well. We went to our family cabin, unpacked, and to the outside deck to have lunch. I kept asking Jay, "are you okay," he replied, "I'm fine." I could tell he was enjoying himself. We had a balcony, and our bed was closed several feet from it. I slept on the side closest to the balcony for safety reasons. When I wanted to sit on the patio, I would grab his hand and view the ocean. As the cruise continued, he was no longer interested in going on the deck. I didn't mind at all. I went on the balcony while he slept during various times on the cruise.

I was so tired I would ask my children to help and set up all our tours. After the second day, my children became very frustrated because they wanted their independence from us. So I complied, and I was on my own handling Jay on the cruise. We tour twice off the boat, and he was well. Shopping going in and out of various shops. Traveling watching the islanders perform outside, no problems. I started to notice while we were on the ship, he became very nervous and agitated. He did not want to leave the cabin. I would continually communicate with him. You love traveling; let's just walk around the ship. We would walk around for about a half-hour. He would say to me." I want to go back," so I returned to the cabin, frustrated every time we attempted to tour the ship. I never let my husband know how distraught I became, however, Dr. Grossman did warn me.

Dinner on the cruise became a challenge. The family and I sat at our assigned table.
Jay would look around and become very jittery in his seat at the table. I was looking around, moving up and down in his chair, and I would touch his hand and tell him to calm down. My children said to me, "Jay doesn't want to be here." They were right! However, I continued to speak to Jay in a calm voice. "We are just going to have our dinner and leave." I looked at the menu and ordered for both of us. The waiter assigned to our table for the five days started to notice Jay's behavior and asked if everything was okay. I assured him everything was fine. Of course, it was not. Here, I am again protecting and lying.

I stopped going to the formal dining area. We continued going on short walks for the rest of the cruise. Sometimes we would sit in a smaller room to eat. Jay was more comfortable in the smaller eatery on the ship. When he was sleeping, one of my children would watch while I toured the boat. A few times, I ate late at night while Jay was in a deep sleep.

Everyone was happy to return home from the cruise. The cruise did not go as well as I desired. Everyone was frustrated, including me; Dr. Grossman was correct.

CHAPTER 7

Suddenly, Reality takes
hold of My Thoughts

I need help to manage my husband and his disease NOW! Is no more necessary, pretending he is okay. He is not well. The various simple things are no longer reality or exist. I have to be more proactive in his care. Jay is at the stage that it's difficult for him to bathe himself. Incontinence has set in. Often in the middle of the night, I was up and changing the linen, bathing and changing Jay. I moved out of our bedroom to another bedroom near the second bathroom down the hallway. That was closer to the stairs so I could get more rest and make sure he did not wander down the stairs in the middle of the night.

I was looking for professional help. The right fit for Jay was very important to me, and I was not going to just put him anywhere. His doctors informed me to put him in a nursing home. I was not ready to give up on him that easily.

So, I enrolled Jay in the Senior Center not far from the house. I had set up Senior Ride Services for him. They picked him up in the morning and dropped him off in the late afternoon. He loves to play pool. At this center, they are involved in games during the day. He played pool all day, and that worked out well in the beginning.

The Senior Center had day trips to various parts of the city. The director wanted the pool group to attend this trip. Thus, I let Jay go on this trip because he was with people that he knew and liked being around.

At the end of my workday, I received a call from the center director informing me that Jay had not returned with the group he was assigned to that day. They all were back
to the bus without him. The leader of the group said that Jay was with the group and then all of a sudden they could not find him. His group thought Jay had headed back to the bus, but he was not there. The bus company was on a time schedule, they had to return to the center. That's when the director of the center called me to inform me what had happened. I thanked her and asked when and where was the last place he was seen.

I called my parents, and my father immediately went to the center. I met him there, and we called the police station in Center City. The director apologized, and I then informed her that Jay has memory complications because I didn't want to go into Jay's full diagnosis. As the director and I were talking, the police pulled up with Jay in the car, and I was so happy. The police said after the description that was given to them. They found him wandering around City Hall. The Senior Center director told me that the center could not be responsible for him, and Jay would no longer be able to attend the Senior Center for liability reasons. I understood and apologized for all the trouble I put the center through.

I was continually in denial and not completely understanding the seriousness of Alzheimer's Disease. However, quickly I was learning. I enrolled Jay in another Senior Center in the suburbs. The center was happy to admit him, and I never mention Jay's diagnoses. To me, most of the time, he handles himself in a normal manner. For the next few weeks, he was managing himself fine. There were no trips outside the center which works out well for me, until one day, in the middle of teaching my class, I received a call from the center. The director said," Mrs. Beckwith, your husband has left the Center. A State Trooper on 309 Highway found your husband walking on the shoulder of 309. A major highway in Cheltenham Montgomery County, Pennsylvania. The Trooper returned him to the center. The Trooper found a paper in his pocket with the center's name on it. We need to speak with you immediately."

When I was home from work, Jay transit van came about 15 minutes after my arrival home. I mentioned to Jay about the 309 incident that happened earlier that day. He had no memory of what happened. I contacted the center, and it was explained to me that the center could not be responsible. "We have noticed other points that need to be addressed. Because of this, we will not be able to accommodate your husband here at this center." I replied, "I understood and apologized," and hung up the phone. I contacted paratransit to stop services until further notice.

I decided after this incident. I immediately filed for Family Leave from my job. This needed to occur to address Jay's medical needs aggressively. Thirty days were approved by my employer. Right away, I found a Daycare Center in the suburbs that only serviced Alzheimer's patients only. I visited the center and loved the setup—clean, activity-driven to keep the clients engaged. The meals are good and nutritional. I only had to make sure Jay had transportation. Therefore, I applied for suburban paratransit pick services that were door to door. I contacted a home nursing service to help me in the morning, giving him breakfast, his medications, and dress him. The home nurse would arrive at 7:15 in the morning. Jay did not like other people to touch him for some reason. So I would have Jay dressed. The nurse addresses the schedule for the morning and puts Jay on the paratransit to the daycare. This helped me to easily transition back to work. Jay got along with the nurse very well. When I went back to work after 30 days, I just would get up earlier to dress Jay, and he would be ready for the nurse to administer his medications and prepare his breakfast when she arrived. I also hired a weekend babysitter to give time to myself, go to the mall, or just give free-time to myself.

One day I was running late for my morning routine. I started to rush, hurrying to dress Jay. I was putting his arms in the sleeves of his shirt and turned around to pick up his cologne. When I turned around, Jay had his right fist in the air, preparing himself to hit me. I immediately said in a calm voice, "Jay, do you really want to hit me." I repeated, "do you really want to hit me!" All of a sudden, the confused evil look on his face was gone. He replied, "I would never hurt you. What is wrong with me." He started to cry. At that moment, we both were crying. I said to him, you will be fine. I realized that I could not rush him. He will become confused and agitated.

The new Alzheimer's Daycare Center was working out well. When I had holidays off doing the week, I would visit the center and observe Jay. He was very happy and enjoyed the various activities, arts and crafts, drawing, puzzles, and engaging small group discussions with one of the staff leading the discussion. He was happy with this center. Finally, I had peace of mind. Jay would come home happy. I kept Jay on a strict schedule, dinner by 6:00 p.m, I showered him, and he was in bed by 8:00 p.m. Sometimes he watched TV until 9:00 p.m.

I received a call one day as I approached the school building for work. It was the Daycare Center's director, "Mrs. Beckwith, the transportation company that drops your husband in the morning leaves immediately after they dropped him off. They are about 10-15 minutes too early. We will not be able to let him enter the center. We will have to let him stand outside." I informed the director that the transportation is only a pickup and drop-off service. Since my husband has been attending for the last two months, there was never a problem. The director replied, "I'm sorry, we will not let him in early. He will have to stand outside." At that point, I was devastated. If he stands outside unsupervised, he will wander off into the woods. Behind the center was nothing but woods. So for the next couple of weeks, I asked his nurse and the paratransit to adjust their schedule. It was fine with the transit company. However, the nurse had another patient when she left my home, and the timing may conflict. She worked it out with the other patient, and it was fine.

Later, Jay started to develop other problems. His fecal incontinence becomes severe to the point I had to shower him in the very early mornings, sometimes 2 a.m. or 3 a.m in the morning. I changed his diet that didn't help. This was another part of the disease I had to deal with him.

One day I had a disagreement with my son. We were standing in the hallway near the steps of the second floor. I thought Jay was in bed. All of a sudden, Jay came from behind me and hit my son in the face so hard that he was falling over the banister head first. I grabbed his sweater, stopping the fall. My son got up, screaming in Jay's face to pull him back. I tried to hold Jay, but they both were too strong for me to control at once. I finally got Jay to return to the bedroom, and I called my sister for help. Then I convince my son to go downstairs. By the time my sister and brother-in-law got to the house, Jay had no memory of what happened. He was asking us why my son was upset. My son was still upset, so my sister asked him to come home with them for the night to calm him down.

Jay has become a threat to himself and the family. The next day, I called one of Jay's neurologists' Dr. Caplan, to explain what happened to my son. His reply was, "Mrs. Beckwith, I told you to put him in a nursing home. It's not going to get any better. That was two years ago, Mrs. Beckwith." Personally, I felt so guilty if I had. That's what I did not want to feel at the time—the guilt of not taking care of my husband.

My deciding factor was that he needed a more restrictive setting. When Jay opens the front door, he wanders out the door. He left one day while I was upstairs. In his mind, he had to move every 15 to 20 minutes. I walked around the neighborhood, but I didn't find him. I was going to call the police when there was a knock on my door. My neighbor down the street returned Jay home. My neighbor said Jay was trying to come to his front door. The model of his home was the same as ours. I thanked my neighbor and told Jay it was time for his shower. Finally, I realized for his safety, it's time to follow the doctor's plan. He needed to be in a more restricted environment, a nursing facility.

The very next day, I visited an Assisted Living facility for Alzheimer's patients about 7 miles from our home. He started out on a day-by-day basis for the first month at $150 a day just to see again if it was a good fit for him. I end up putting him there full time, and he continued his stay there for a year. Jay was becoming very combative and did not want anyone to shower him. After working a full day, every evening, I was there showing my husband. He would not let anyone else do it. I was only seven miles away, but still, I was exhausted, but no one else could do it. Also, I brought his clothes home every week for laundry and ironed them. The facility loses his clothes, or they were in someone else's room.

The assisted living facility complained about Jay's combativeness. One early morning, I received a call from a worker at 2 a.m. in the morning, complaining my husband can't sleep. He just wants to sit in the activity room. And when she tried to insist on him to go back to his room, and she touches his upper arm to help him, Jay snapped his arm back and, with an evil look on his face, said, "do not touch me." The worker said, "Mrs. Beckwith, I need you to come up and help me get your husband back to his room." My reply to her was, "no. It's 2 a.m. in the morning, and the staff are trained to handle situations. I placed my husband in a facility that only admitted patients with memory problems and Alzheimer's. I was told that all the patient behaviors would be addressed properly. Now you call me to get out of bed and come there to help you. I am sorry I will not." Then I hung up the phone. The next day, I called the director and told her about the incident. She apologized and said," at times, your husband does have his difficult times here." I replied, "you have all his medical records. His behavior is not a surprise. And I might add, this facility said you are used to this type of behavior, and staff are trained to handle various behaviors.

The problems start with this facility. When Jay became very combative, the facility informed me they would put him for a time at another location to work on his aggressiveness for his safety and others. Jay was sent there twice at different times while staying at assisted living. When his behavior became too difficult for them to handle, I consented for Jay to stay there.

I visited Jay there both times, he seemed to recognize me and give eye contact. He was very quiet and that "Alz Face" suddenly appeared. From that moment, there was no eye contact, just the stare. I realized it was time for me to leave. I informed the staff, and they carefully take him back to his room.

The second time I brought along with me a handheld tape recorder. Jay loves music, so I thought this would be great communication while visiting Jay. Jay loved music, Spiritual, Classical, Jazz, and Contemporary music. He played the piano and was in a band before we met. When we were first married, he often spoke about how much he loved playing in the band. He had a framed picture of himself and three other musicians that he was very proud to show off among friends.

I was right, I put the headphones over his head, adjusted the volume, and the expression on his face changed. A smile appeared on his face, and I escorted him to the hallway. The music was a calming tool for Jay. He briefly remembered his past, Music! When I watched him walk up and down the hallway singing along with a happy look continually on his face, that look too made me happy as well. When it was time to go, I asked him if I could have the recorder back. Surprisingly he handed it over to me very calmly with a smile.

After each visit, Jay was admitted back to the assisted living facility after a few days. A month after his last return, he had become very dehydrated. I took him to the University Of Pennsylvania Emergency Room, and he stayed in the hospital for a week. During that time, Dr. Grossman had the social service department find a nursing home facility. The neurology and social services departments told me it was time to put him in the nursing facility to get better medical care. After looking over several nursing homes, they finally found one I approved of. He was released in a week straight to the nursing home in Lansdale, Pennsylvania.

CHAPTER 8

Caregivers, Sometimes Fail To Think Of Themselves.

Running around making sure my husband's medical needs were met, unfortunately, I totally neglected my health; my eating habits, high blood pressure, and extreme fatigue. I desperately needed a change of scenery, some quality time to myself. My blood pressure became so high, and my primary care doctor referred me to a cardiologist. The cardiologist immediately put me on the highest hypertension medication.

My weight was out of control. Instead of cooking, I purchased fast food. At the time, it was convenient because I was doing a great deal of running around. From my job everyday teaching to visiting Jay's facility helping to address his needs every day, and staying on top of running my limo business. Before I knew it, I had gained 30 pounds. The weight continued to pile on.

Years prior, I was diagnosed with asthma. However, I had it under control until now. I started to have asthma attacks at work and at home. At work, I was outside for a fire drill with my students. The wind blew, immediately I started coughing and couldn't catch my breath. Another teacher noticed I was gasping for air, so she called the nurse. I refused when asked to let them call 911. I insisted in a low, quiet voice. "I want to sit quietly at the rear of my classroom. I'll be fine." The teacher's aide stood in front of my class, reviewing my last lesson. While I sat at the rear of the classroom for 30 minutes until my breathing became normal again, I remembered having attacks at home. One of the attacks was so severe, 911 had to be called again. When the EMTs arrived at my home, they had to work on me to get my breathing under control first, then transport me to the hospital. The home incident happened to me twice. I always waited before I called 911, thinking I could get my asthma under control. My primary doctor was also my asthma specialist. She informed me she had a patient that always waited before calling 911. The patient died thinking she had it under control. My doctor informed me so I would stop playing with my life. Her concern warranting definitely frightened me. I followed her direction explicitly and subsequently.

We had two lovable miniature poodles, Fris and Polo. They are part of the family. You can say they were like little humans running around our home, groomed every six weeks faithfully. I never missed an appointment. One day my twin came to visit and noticed Fris and Polo's hair was so long. She asked, "When was the last time you had them groomed?" I answered, "about 3 months. Jay's care has completely taken over my life." I could no longer care for them properly. Eventually, I had them groomed. And came to the conclusion that I needed to find them a better home.. I can't attend to their needs as I use to. A loving home for Fris and Polo was found in a few weeks.

Depression had set in, and I was so overwhelmed with everything in my life. My life was falling apart. It came to the point I was afraid to answer my phone. I knew at the other end of the phone, I needed to do something for Jay. Or address Jay's medical condition or bills. There was always something that needed my immediate attention. I couldn't work with a clear mind. One day, as I walked toward the school building to start my workday. My cell phone rang. I stopped just before opening the school's door and turned around and said hello. The voice on the other end, Mrs. Beckwith, I am Ms. -------, the director of the Alzheimer's Daycare Center. Your husband arrives at the center too early, 15-20 minutes before our doors open in the mornings. He will have to stand outside." I replied, "is he safe in the building now?" She said, "'yes." I told her I am at work. I will discuss this further after work. I signed in at the front desk, went to the vice principal's office, and started to cry. The vice-principal felt so bad for me that she covered my classes for two hours so I could pull myself together. I had a headache, and I knew my blood pressure was slowly creeping up. I had to get myself together.

My doctor visit was unpleasant. I am ashamed of how I totally let my health deteriorate. My doctor, this particular day, took more time with me after I had explained to her in more detail what was presently going on in my life. She knew about Jay's Alzheimer's. She explained that I must take care of myself first. Or everything, my health, Jay's health, finances, all I worked for will go down the drain. She started by telling me to start eating better again. I needed to think about putting Jay in a more restrictive environment. Go back and consult your attorney again about my financial options.

After her taking the time to speak to me about everything that was going on with me, I started to cry uncontrollably. That day, the doctor let me sit in the patient's exam room for over an hour. She asked her nurses to use the other patient's exam rooms for her other patients.

Caring for yourself is very important. Occasionally, you can slip into depression and not realize it until you are right in the middle of depression. One day I was in the middle of the floor screaming, "What is going on with me." I just received a phone call about the medical bill for Jay that I missed because I didn't have the funds to pay the bill. I politely thanked the other person on the phone and hung up the phone. The moment I put the phone down, I started screaming. I was screaming so loud my son ran down the stairs into the kitchen, where I was standing in the middle of the floor. "I can't take this.!" Backing into the corner with hands holding my head. My son called out to me. Mom, are you okay? I looked at him, screaming, "No! I don't know what else to do." I kept screaming. "I don't know what else to do" I wouldn't move out of the corner. My son said he was going to call my daughter, who was out of town attending school. I told him I would be fine. I need some time. Just let me have some time alone. I need time to figure out how I was going to pay Jay's medical bill.

He said, "okay, I'll be in my room." I stood in that corner for about an hour. I decided to keep moving. I will figure it out.

Caregiving is a great contribution to our family or the person you are helping. However, you are doing a great injustice to your health and wellbeing if you are not taking care of yourself. When you fly, before the airplane leaves the airport, the flight attendant will instruct you, if there's an emergency, to put your oxygen mask on first. Then put the oxygen mask on your child or someone who requires assistance. Always stay focused on your physical and mental health. You can't help anyone if you are depressed and unhealthy.

Various Self-Care Practices

*Apply for various Grants
Contact local, state, and national Alzheimer's Association
for direction
*SeniorAssistanceBenefits.org - Get information about how to apply for
benefits
Helpful Information About Senior Benefits

*Virtue Shopping
Grocery and clothing shopping
* Outside help to do your laundry
*Healthy Prepared Meals Delivery services
Meal kit companies over-ready meals
Ready-made smoothies and slice fruits
* Help with your home cleaning and organization
* Home Exercise Program
* Mediation
*Regular conversations with friends or family members
*Hire an adult caregiver for a day. To allow yourself entertainment and
enjoy yourself.

Advance Health Care Directives And Living Wills

When planning for your future medical care, prepare your advance directives to be sure your loved ones make health choices according to your wishes. Each state has forms there to address your request.aarp. org/AdvanceDirectiveForms. Over 60 percent of Americans who haven't prepared any life care documents, there is no time like the present to put your wishes on paper. And if you have already created advance directives and designated a health care surrogate or proxy, go and review your documents and determine whether they need to be updated for a reason. If your documents are older than five years, consider making new ones.

CHAPTER 9

Immediate Cause Of Your Financial Adjustments. As The Alzheimer's Disease Progresses, Your Finances Aren't Strictly Your Own Anymore

Right away, I seek legal help. I immediately contacted my attorney, which had previously done our Family Will years prior. My attorney explained the process for Nursing Homes and Assisted Living Facilities. He said I was in the time frame and that the Laws for the care facilities were about to change in the next year. However, everything was presented in my favor, and the attorney informed me that there is a financial "Look Back," meaning the facilities will look at your assets and require you to relinquish your assets to them. The "Look Back" provision at that time was three years. In less than a year, the law will change to 5 years "Look Back" [8]
The attorney started the paperwork at once. I signed off, and when everything is done, he would call me to look it over and address any questions I may have.

We also discuss how to address all of Jay's saving accounts and 401k. My attorney informed me I could get $235 a month for life from my husband's pension. I immediately refused. I told my attorney I want his

---

[8] Google defines Financial resources for nursing, service or private in-home service out of pocket.

full retirement to be used for his care. Please let that stay in place to help with medical and housing expenses. However, I was advised to withdraw everything from the savings account and purchase items that were needed, and pay off bills. I promptly did exactly what I was told. He assured me that this was all legal in the parameters of the law. I was very relieved to have an attorney look out for my best interest.

There was a time when one of my sister's coworkers told me to divorce my husband for financial reasons and continue to take care of him. The divorce was only to protect our assets. I did not want to go down that path. She was very persistent for me to follow up on her suggestion. I thanked her, but I did not consider the suggestion.

When Jay first became ill, I had a Codicil[9] draw up to our Will that his older sister will take care of him and manage his assets if something happens to me, and she agreed. After a few months, she started to make various demands of various information about the house, and Jay should be buried in Florida on and on.

Immediately, I revoke my decision about his oldest sister, and I updated my will for my children to handle everything. I never told Jay's oldest sister that I removed her from our will.

---

[9] Codicil is a testamentary document similar but not necessarily identical to a Will. Some jurisdictions may serve to amend, rather than a replacement, previously executed will. -WIKIPEDIA

CHAPTER 10

The Last Six Months Of His Life Were Slowly Devastating, Numbing, Helpless

A call came in the middle of the day. It was the Hospice Service at Jay's nursing home. The director wanted to speak to me about putting Jay into hospice. I quickly responded, "I have no interest in putting my husband in hospice; I'm on the job. Could you please call me after 4 pm?" She agreed, once I was home, she called me right on time. I sat down in the chair in my living room, and I immediately said to the director, "your staff are giving up on my husband's care. My understanding of hospice is just let him die." For me, to make that decision is devastating. Instantly, the director said to me. "Mrs. Beckwith, hospice care is to make the patient as comfortable as possible. Hospice care is not always permanent or the end of someone's life. Many patients come out of hospice. We are here to make Mr. Beckwith's stay more comfortable. You can also decide to do the hospice at home and not here at this facility. I informed the director I would think about our conversation and get back to her.

Heart Failure and Alzheimer's Disease

Dementia and heart failure (HF) both represent growing social, healthcare, and economic problems. It is estimated that there were more than 35 million people worldwide with dementia in 2010, and this number is expected to double every 20 years.

1) largely due to a population but also to an increasing prevalence of risk factors for dementia. The annual worldwide cost of dementia was 604 billion dollars in 2010

2). The most common form of dementia is Alzheimer's disease (AD), and the major risk factor for its development is increasing age.

3) Other known risk factors include family history, hypertension and hypotension, high cholesterol levels, low levels of physical activity and of education, obesity, and the presence of epsilon 4 allele of the apolipoprotein E gene (APOE4) 4- 6. A recently proposed risk factor for AD is HF 7.

Chronic Heart Failure (HF) is a progressive condition defined as an inadequate cardiac output to meet metabolic demands. The most common causes of HF in developed countries include ischaemic heart disease with myocardial infarction, hypertension, cardiomyopathy and degenerative, valve disorders.

The prevalence of HF is about 2% 8, increasing sharply with age, with up to 10% of individuals over 65 years 8, and 20% over 75 years affected 9. It has been shown that HF is more 'malignant' cancer overall 9. Hospitalization for HF accounts for 1-2% of all healthcare expenditures in Europe 10, and HR is the most common cause of hospitality in patients over 65 years of age 11.

Alzheimer's disease and HF often occur together and thus increase the cost of care and health resource utilization 12; this highlights the need to investigate the relationship between these two conditions. Impaired cognition in HF patients leads to significantly more frequent hospital readmissions 13 and increases mortality rates 14 The relation between HF and AD remains largely unclear. In this review, we aim to explain how HF contributes to the development of AD, focusing mainly on reduced cerebral blood flow(CBF) 15 and dysfunction of the neurovascular unit 16. However, multiple cardiovascular conditions often coexist, suggesting that several mechanisms underlying cardiovascular dysfunction may contribute to cognitive decline. HF in the elderly is often underdiagnosed because the symptoms of HF are mimicked or masked by comorbidities in this population. 17. Causes of HF and common comorbidities will be discussed with emphasis on their contribution to dementia and specifically AD.

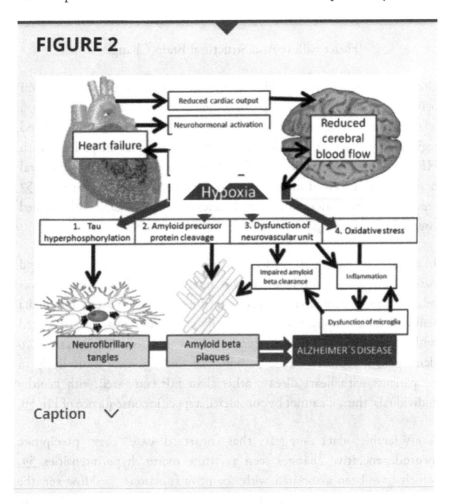

FIGURE 2

Caption ∨

Early identification and correct medical treatment of cardiovascular conditions can reduce the prevalence of AD 18. Indeed prevention of AD may be more effective than current pharmacological treatment 19,20. It has been estimated that delaying the onset of AD by just one year would lead to 9 million fewer cases by 2050 21. During the past three years, the results of at least five studies have been published, suggesting that the incidence of dementia and AD may have decreased over the last two decades 22-26. The mortality improvements are attributed to better awareness of cardiovascular disease risk factors. Besides, successful management of hypertension and an increase in statins and antithrombotic drugs may play an important role.

Heart Failure And Structural Brain Changes

Growing evidence from neuroimaging studies suggests an association between HF and structural brain abnormalities, further supporting a relationship between dysfunction of both the heart and brain. Total and regional brain atrophy or demyelination are common in patients with HF [50]; Kumar and colleagues found reduced axon integrity of several brain circuits involved in cognition in these patients [51]. Serber et al. [52] reported abnormalities of the frontal cortex, which correlated with reduced cognitive functioning.

In a study comparing HF patients with both healthy control subjects and patients diagnosed with heart disease other HF, it is found that HF was related to more white matter hyperintensities, lacunar infarcts, and media temporal lobe atrophy. Medial is an early feature of AD and is associated with lower cognitive function and an increased risk of progression to dementia.[53]. However, these pathological findings were more likely to be patients with heart disease other than HF compared with healthy individuals, thus, it cannot be considered a specific consequence of HF [50].

Considerable data suggest that heart disease may precipitate neurodegenerative changes seen as white matter hyperintensities [54], which have been associated with cognitive functions [55]. However, the clinical significance of these changes is not clear, as they are widespread in the elderly population, and many studies are not related to cognitive performance [56,57].

FIGURE 3

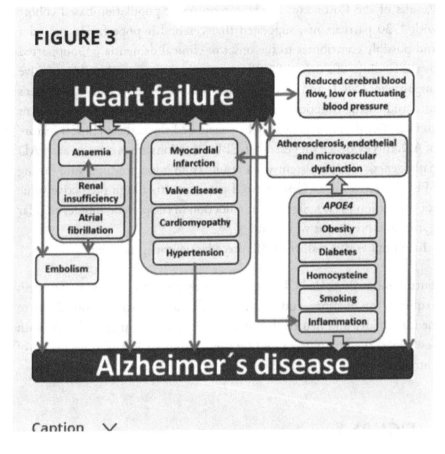

Caption ⌄

Cerebral Blood Flow (CBF) In
Alzheimer's Disease

It has been demonstrated extensively that vascular changes and reduced blood supply of the brain are involved in Alzheimer's Disease58. There is a large body of evidence indicating that AD is characterized by a reduction in both and regional CBF with resulting brain hypoperfusion. Total CBF is about 20% lower in patients with Alzheimer's disease compared with individuals without dementia 15. Lower CBF has been reported and confirmed in many studies using single-photon emission computed tomography (SPECT), positron tomography, spin labeling magnetic resonance imaging (MRI), or transcranial Doppler measurements 59-61. It seems likely that reduced CBF can cause neuronal dysfunction or death 62.

Results of the Rotterdam Study, a prospective population-based cohort with 1730 participants, suggested that cerebral hypoperfusion precedes and possibly contributes to the onset of clinical dementia <u>63.</u> Supported by the findings of a delay in CBF response in patients with mild cognitive impairment (MCI) and an even longer delay in patients with Alzheimer's in a study using functional MRI and blood oxygenation level-dependent contrast <u>64.</u> Because MCI may be considered the earliest clinical feature of AD, this evidence suggests that CBF reductions are present in early AD pathogenesis. It's consistent with results from a longitudinal study using SPECT to investigate CBF in MCI patients with a high predictive value for conversion to AD. Significant reduction in the parietal lobule, angular gyrus, and precuneus was found <u>65,</u>
which implies that reduced CBF precedes neurodegeneration.

Furthermore, decreased CBF may negatively affect the synthesis of protein required for memory and learning and may eventually contribute to neuritic injury and neuronal death [66]. It has been suggested that brain low blood flow may be caused by the continuous loss of innervation of intracerebral blood vessels [67].

FIGURE 1

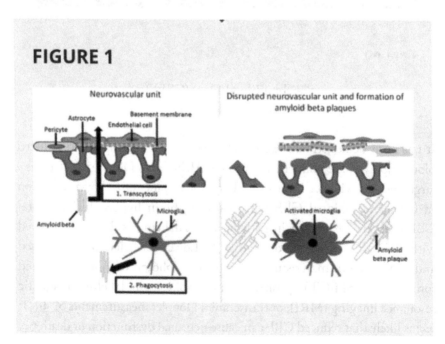

I visited Jay every day ever since he was placed in the nursing home facility. No matter where the facility is located, I was there. Over the next few months, Jay developed a Congestive Heart Failure, and his body was slowly shutting down. His daily activities had changed. He utilized the activity room, playing games, and walking around. All of a sudden, the daily activities stopped. He had become more confined to his room. We used to engage in small talk and go to the facility outside the sitting area.. Jay no longer had interest in doing those simple things with me anymore. He had stopped eating solid foods at the facility. He was only given liquid, the hospice nurse informed me. I requested the nursing home facility to take my husband back to the University of Pennsylvania Health System to see Dr. Grossman for a clinical examination. Dr. Grossman's finding;

John Beckwith for follow-up Consultation On November 13, 2007
To The Nursing Home Physician

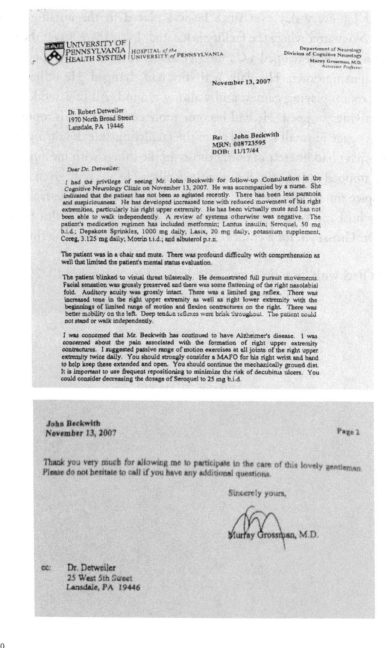

Department of Neurology
Division of Cognitive Neurology
Murray Grossman, M.D.
Associate Professor

November 13, 2007

Dr. Robert Detweiler
1970 North Broad Street
Lansdale, PA 19446

Re: John Beckwith
MRN: 008723595
DOB: 11/17/44

Dear Dr. Detweiler:

I had the privilege of seeing Mr. John Beckwith for follow-up Consultation in the Cognitive Neurology Clinic on November 13, 2007. He was accompanied by a nurse. She indicated that the patient has not been as agitated recently. There has been less paranoia and suspiciousness. He has developed increased tone with reduced movement of his right extremities, particularly his right upper extremity. He has been virtually mute and has not been able to walk independently. A review of systems otherwise was negative. The patient's medication regimen has included metformin; Lantus insulin; Seroquel, 50 mg b.i.d.; Depakote Sprinkles, 1000 mg daily; Lasix, 20 mg daily; potassium supplement, Coreg, 3.125 mg daily; Motrin t.i.d.; and albuterol p.r.n.

The patient was in a chair and mute. There was profound difficulty with comprehension as well that limited the patient's mental status evaluation.

The patient blinked to visual threat bilaterally. He demonstrated full pursuit movements. Facial sensation was grossly preserved and there was some flattening of the right nasolabial fold. Auditory acuity was grossly intact. There was a limited gag reflex. There was increased tone in the right upper extremity as well as right lower extremity with the beginnings of limited range of motion and flexion contractures on the right. There was better mobility on the left. Deep tendon reflexes were brisk throughout. The patient could not stand or walk independently.

I was concerned that Mr. Beckwith has continued to have Alzheimer's disease. I was concerned about the pain associated with the formation of right upper extremity contractures. I suggested passive range of motion exercises at all joints of the right upper extremity twice daily. You should strongly consider a MAFO for his right wrist and hand to help keep these extended and open. You should continue the mechanically ground diet. It is important to use frequent repositioning to minimize the risk of decubitus ulcers. You could consider decreasing the dosage of Seroquel to 25 mg b.i.d.

**John Beckwith
November 13, 2007**

Page 2

Thank you very much for allowing me to participate in the care of this lovely gentleman. Please do not hesitate to call if you have any additional questions.

Sincerely yours,

Murray Grossman, M.D.

cc: Dr. Detweiler
25 West 5th Street
Lansdale, PA 19446

10

---

[10] **Results of John B. Beckwith**
GROSS DESCRIPTION of his Brain Autopsy #: A07-248
Atrophic brain consistent with clinical diagnosis of Alzheimer's Disease

The medical decision to stop giving him fluids was because he could no longer swallow. I was again highly upset. The hospice nurse calms me down to say, "Mrs. Beckwith, if we continue giving him fluids, he will choke to death because he has lost the ability to swallow." I realized Jay's body was slowly shutting down. I consented for them to stop the fluids. My first thought was to bring him home and have the hospice services there. Jay loved the house so much the way he would nurture and made sure everything was flowing properly will make his time more comfortable at home. I had planned to put a hospital bed in the family room. I called my twin sister, Janet, and my father, to tell them about my plans. They both disagreed and asked me to reconsider bringing him home. They were looking out for me. They knew It would stress me even more. After speaking to them, I decided not to bring him home.

I called his family in Florida to let them know that he is now in hospice. His father thanked me for taking care of his son. He could not come to Philadelphia to see Jay. He was in his mid-90's. But, Jay's father visited him twice before his diagnosis. I strongly suggested to Jay's father not to come to Philadelphia. I promised him that I would keep him informed of his son's condition. Jay has five siblings, three sisters and two brothers. Jay was next to the youngest; they all lived in Florida. The older sister always tried to make demands to know about Jay's care, but she never came up to visit her brother. She said, "she wanted to remember Jay how he was before he became sick." His two brothers and middle-sister visited Philadelphia a few times before Jay's diagnosis and once after his diagnosis. The youngest sister never visited because she said," she couldn't afford the flight to Philadelphia."

It was Thanksgiving, 2007. I had Thanksgiving Dinner at my youngest sister's home in Yeadon, PA. We had finished dinner, sitting around chatting. I looked at my father and said, "Dad, I have to go. I want to visit Jay before I go home." My father said, "I think you need to skip the visit tonight. You look very tired to do that tonight. Too long of a drive for you tonight." I thought about it; he was right. The distance is 1 hour and 24 minutes from my location, and I was exhausted. So, I spent a little more time with my family and left, and went straight home.

I remembered that I had made an appointment with our funeral director the next day just to get the arrangements out of the way. I was very tired by the time I reached home. I thought about what my father had said. My father was right. I'm too tired. I took a shower and went to bed.

I had awakened about 6:15 a.m. and looked at my clock. I was lying on my right side and felt this weird force holding me for about twenty seconds. Then my phone rang. It was the nursing home informing that Jay had passed at 6:15 a.m. I was dazed. I called my father and my twin sister Janet. My father asked me if I was okay. "I just need to contact our Funeral Director to pick up Jay's remains," I replied.

I contacted the funeral director. I had made an appointment last week to make arrangements for Jay's final resting place ahead of time. I called the funeral director, when he realized it was me, he confirmed our appointment for that afternoon. I then responded, "he passed this morning. Could you please pick up Jay's remains?" He said, "yes, no problem." I gave him the address of the nursing home facility. I then explained to him I was donating Jay's Brain to Science at the University Of Pennsylvania Neurology Department for study to help other Alzheimer's patients. And please keep that information confidential. He assured me that he would take care of everything and not to worry. And he did, very professionally.

My twin sister and her husband were shopping for Black Friday sales. They immediately left the mall and came to my home, and volunteered to drive me to the nursing home facility. When we arrived at the nursing facility, I walked toward Jay's room. The funeral director was standing in the hallway outside Jay's room. "Mrs. Beckwith, I was waiting here for your arrival." I thanked him again and walked into Jay's room. My sister and brother-in-law stood in the hallway, talking to the funeral director. I proceed to Jay's bedside. He looked like he was so much at peace finally. All the suffering he had gone through for the last five years. He has stepped back from and been released. No more suffering. Surprisingly, I didn't break down and cry. I was very sad and hurt. However, the relief that his body-mind continues to deteriorate and I could no longer help has given me unselfish peace too as his caregiver.

My sister and brother-in-law, after a while, walked into Jay's room to check on me. I told them I was fine. I walked out to speak to the funeral director. As I was talking to him, I heard my twin crying. I was trying very hard to keep the focus on the conversation with the funeral director. I signed the necessary paperwork he had with him and made an appointment to meet with him the next day to finalize Jay's arrangements.

My son came over to spend the night—the next morning at around 4 a.m., I woke up to take my son to work at the mall; after dropping him off, I headed back home. About two miles from home, a herd of about seven deer crossed the street about two cars ahead of me. We all stopped to let them cross. When I drove across that point, one deer out of nowhere had broadsided the right side of the front right fender. I stopped again. The deer continued to run across the street. I continued home without stopping until I reached my driveway. I looked at the damages with no feeling whatsoever. I called the insurance company and informed them about my accident, and when I went to bed. That afternoon I drove to the funeral home to finalize Jay's funeral arrangements.

Jay was laid to rest on December 5, 2007, in Philadelphia, Pennsylvania. John Benjamin Beckwith was now at peace.

The results from John Benjamin Beckwith Autopsy.

Gross Description of the Brain

Name: Beckwith, John   Autopsy #: A07-248

Sex: Male   Race: Black

GROSS DESCRIPTION:

The brain was examined 11 hours postmortem and it weighs 948 grams. Both external and internal surfaces of the dural leaflets are smooth and free from nodules. The superior sagittal sinus is patent. The external surfaces of the brain are symmetric and exhibit moderate atrophy without softening or discoloration. There is no evidence of herniation of the cingulate gyri, uncus or cerebellar tonsils. The leptomeninges are thin translucent and free from exudate. Examination of the arteries of the Circle of Willis and their major branches reveals that they are patent, without atherosclerosis. The superficial veins of the brain are unremarkable.

Serial coronal sections reveal atrophic cortex and centrum ovale. The cerebral cortex has an average thickness of 3-4 mm. The ventricles are symmetrical and moderately dilated. There is no deviation of the septum pellucidum. There is no evidence of infarction, hemorrhage, or tumor mass. The nuclei of the brain, including the thalami, the caudate, the lentiform, the lateral geniculate bodies and the subthalamic nuclei are unremarkable. The hippocampus and amygdala are small. The substantia nigra is unremarkable and the locus ceruleus is depigmented. The internal capsules, the cerebral peduncles, the pons, the medulla, the cerebellar hemispheres, the vermis and the cerebellar nuclei are all unremarkable. A 2 cm segment of the cervical spinal cord is available for examination. Portions of the left and right hemisphere are fixed in ethanol and neutral buffered formalin for microscopic examination, while other portions are frozen.

GROSS DIAGNOSIS: Atrophic brain consistent with clinical diagnosis of Alzheimer's disease

Date: 11.23.07

Staff, Fellows, Residents:
Mark S. Forman, M.D., Ph.D.
John Q. Trojanowski, M.D., Ph.D.

11

Two days after Jay's funeral, I had two phone calls. My gynecologist called me about the mammogram results, that I had an abnormal screening. I

11

needed to schedule a more precise screening. The second call was from my attorney to attend a hearing that the Assisted Living facility was suing me.

I was so numb from what I had been through in the last month. I just could not react. The appointments happen to be on the same day—the court hearing in the morning, mammogram screening in the afternoon. A week later, sitting in the hearing, my attorney defended my case about the "Look Back" provision. I won the case. The court ruled that all my paperwork was filed in time before the law changed from 3 years to 5 years.

From the hearing, I proceeded straight to a different mammogram location for a colored imaging screening. My results, thank God, were negative, with no sign of cancer cells. After those incidents. I started to slowly put my life back together.

CHAPTER 11

Bereavement

Bereavement is the period after a loss during which grief is experienced and mourning occurs. The time spent in a period of bereavement depends on how attached the person was to the person who died, and how much time was spent anticipating the loss.[12]

The loss of Jay's was challenging, to say the least. I did not cry, but I was deeply detached from myself and my environment. I was a Functioning Robot. I lost my mother 4 years prior. Two months before she passed, she asked, "what do you want for your birthday?" I said, Just hold me, mom. I repeated it again. "Just hold me; that's all I want." She was the person I always confide in about Jay's Alzheimer's. My mother and father were still there for me. When my mother suddenly had a stroke, I didn't feel the grief. I didn't have the opportunity to grieve her death. I went back into caregiving mode. I realized something was not right with me. Three months into the following year after Jay's passing, a friend recommended me to attend group grief counseling with her. She came to my home to pick me up, and I reluctantly attended the meeting. I sat down in the rear of the room. The seating was set up in a circle, and I was asked to join them in the circle. I told the grief counselor I was fine where I was seated. I listened to everyone else's story. I was asked just before the meeting was over did I want to say something. I replied, "no." The following week, I

---

[12] **Alzheimer's Association**

went back. This time I sat in the circle. I listen to others' stories. I was asked again if I would like to say something. This time I said my name and told them my husband died. It's time for me to return to work. I was afraid to return to work because I didn't want anyone to ask me questions or mention anything about his death. I am trying to get the strength to return back to work. All of a sudden, I started to cry uncontrollably. I said," I can't be here, I need to leave." The meeting soon ended. I was still crying. I tried to stop, but I could not. The grief counselor came over to me and said she was willing to help me one-on-one if that was better for me, and I could call her if I had trouble adjusting once I returned to work. Within a couple of days, I was back at work. I did call in the middle of my workday. I told her so far I was fine. I would like to see her one-on-one weekly. In our sessions, it was established that I was grieving my mother.

Ways To Cope With Grief And Loss

• Face your feelings.
  Think about all of your feelings---positive and negative. Let yourself be as sad as you want, and accept the feeling of guilt because they are normal. Work through your anger and frustration. These are healthy emotions. Know that it is common to feel love and anger at the same time.

*Prepare to experience feelings of loss more than once.
It is common to go through feelings of grief and
loss again. Accept and acknowledge your feelings. They are a normal part of the grieving process.

* Claim the grieving process as your own.
No two people experience grief the same way. Grief hits different people at times; some people need more time to grieve than others. Your experience will depend on the severity and duration of the person's illness, on your own history of loss, and on the nature of your relationship with the person who has Alzheimer's or other forms of loss.

*Speak with someone about your grief friend, family member or
a professional counselor

Talk with someone you trust about your grief, guilt, and anger. If you decide
with a therapist/counselor who specializes in grief counseling, you should
consider someone you are comfortable to express your deepest feelings

* Online counseling is available for those individuals with hectic schedules.
Could select getting help without leaving home or caregiving living space

*Combat feelings of isolation and loneliness.
Caregivers often give up enjoyable activities and companionship. Make
a lunch or movie date with friends. Taking a break may help you relieve
stress and grief and strengthen your support network. Stay involved in
activities that you enjoy.

*Join a support group.
When you talk with other caregivers, share your emotion, cry and laugh
together, do not limit conversations to caregiving tips. Alzheimer's
Associate Support groups take place all across the country. Find one near
you. If you prefer online support, join ALZConnected, an online caregiver
community with message boards.

*Know that some people may not understand your grief.
Most people think grief happens when someone dies. They may not know
that it is possible to grieve deeply for someone who has a progressive
cognitive illness?

*Accept yourself.
Think about what you expect from yourself. Is it realistic?
Learn to accept the things that are beyond your control.
Make responsible decisions about the things you can control.

*Take care of yourself.
The best thing you can do for the person you are caring for is to stay
healthy, and this includes taking care of your physical, mental, emotional
well-being. Create balance in your life. Do things that bring joy and
comfort, and give yourself time to rest. Ask for help when you need it and
accept the help that's offered.

CHAPTER 12

References For Various Behavior Changes

Symptoms Of Dementia /Alzheimer's Disease

1. Driving a vehicle becomes erratic

    a. Not obeying traffic signs or lights
    b. The noise of surrounding traffic
        1. The blowing of a vehicle horn
        2. The sound a vehicle racing
    c. Forgetting the original destination while driving
    d. Forgetting how to fuel your vehicle
    e. Forgetting how to operate a vehicle

3. Not managing their personal or family finances

    a. All of a sudden, not recalling to pay bills or forgetting how to
    b. Difficult and confusing, learning new ways of banking
        1. Direct Deposit
        2. Accessing Your Funds Quickly
    c. Changing personal or family documents with no recall of it happening

3. Recall of various earlier conversations not remembered

    a. Counting backward
      1. Can't do accurately
      2. Ask to count and remember two objects before counting.
        After counting can't recall the 2-3 objects

4. *No longer interested in their favorite hobby or adventure*

    a. Traveling/Vacations becomes challenging
    b. Hobbies are very difficult to do that once was very easy to do.

5. Old memories are more present (10-30 years prior) than the present moment.

6. Deciding how to dress

    a. No longer able to shop for clothing
    b. What to wear is more a challenge than normal
    c. Confusing what piece of clothing goes whereas they dress themselves

7. Normally calm, all of a sudden patience, concise, low tolerance level

8. Forgetting to use the bathroom

    a. Bed wetting at night. Eventually full incontinence

9. Showering/bathing themselves becomes challenging

    a. Claiming a shower/bath was done but had not
    b. Forgetting how to shower/bathe themselves
    c. Shaving constantly cutting themselves than normal

10. Leaving appliances on in the Kitchen

    a. The stove is left on while cooking. Leave the kitchen, never recalling something left on the stove.
    b. Refrigerator doors are wide open
    c. Kitchen Faucet left on
    d. Various appliances that were normally used in the kitchen, can't remember how to use them.

11. In denial of the changes in their mental/physical health

    a. At the beginning of the diagnoses refuses to accept the diagnosis
    b. Refuse to address health issues
        1. Can't remember to take medications

12. Constantly losing personal items

    a. Wallet
    b. Keys
    c. Something of value to them

13. Stop remembering family faces and names

14. Combativeness

    a. Refuses to comply often with daily hygiene
        1. Could become very angry
        2. Sometimes violent
    b. Do not like to be rushed or hurried along
    c. Some cases trusted only to a familiar face
        1. May become combative during activities
    d. Easily become anointed and argumentative for no apparent reason

15. Storing items in various places in their home. Not remembering why it was stored there.

16. Confusion on the job/home

    a. Forgetting responsibilities on the job
    b. Their performance on the job is erratic
    c. Disoriented at home when it comes to regular household chores

17. Attending regular activities and gathering socially with friends cease to exist

    a. No longer recognize friends and previous activities. No longer interested in communicating or interacting

18. 18.Wandering

    a. Can no longer sit for long periods of time
    b. Will walk to unfamiliar and dangerous places
        1. Will not comprehend how dangerous it is
          Ex. Walking on to a highway, an intersection, or a stranger's property, etc.

Pandemic Preparations

Neurodegenerative diseases are conditions of the brain and/or spinal cord, where a progressive loss of brain cells causes problems with memory, thinking, and/or movement. When memory and thinking problems are severe enough to make the person dependent on others, this is called dementia. The most common causes of dementia are Alzheimer's disease, stroke, or vascular; this is called cognitive impairment, Parkinson's disease, frontotemporal dementia, and amyotrophic lateral sclerosis or ALS.

Pandemics are a challenge to our society and health care system, but there are some easy things we can do to ensure the health and well-being of some of the most vulnerable members of our society-those living with dementia, stroke, and neurodegenerative disease.

Example include:

1. Use technology.
    (a) Many hospitals and primary care organizations may limit people access, but options for telephone calls and/or computer visits are quickly being established. Doctors are being asked to provide more care through phone calls and video technology, but we must ensure patients can benefit. Where possible, people should make efforts to ensure vulnerable populations have the technology (like iPads for virtual visits) and that they understand how to use it.
    (b) Caregivers and families can help to ensure vulnerable elderly have devices and access to the internet to connect to care providers and potentially avoid hospitals or offices without sacrificing care. Similarly, family and friends may also have to limit in-person contact but could be more available for phone or video visits. Where available, online ordering for or medication may make it easier to avoid long lines.

2. Make sure you have enough but don't stockpile medications.

    We all need to ensure we have a sufficient supply of medications to reduce the need to make trips to the pharmacy. Many pharmacies will also deliver, so those at increased risk may wish to consider this as an alternative. However, according to the Canadian Pharmacists Association," unnecessary stockpiling of medication creates unintended shortages and puts other patients' health at risk."

3. Know your resources and seek support. Familiarize yourself with support agencies in your community and know how to reach them. There are many organizations, including Heart & Stroke, the Alzheimer's Society, ALS Society, Parkinson's Foundation, Memory Clinic, Regional Geriatric Programs. For people living with or caring for someone with dementia, or Alzheimer's, contact the Alzheimer's Association. These will help offer many services.

The Alzheimer's Association 7/24 Hotline(800.272.3900)
web: ALZ.org
For Heart & Stroke emergency: call 911 immediately.

For general question
Heart Disease - Management and recovery

Find health publications
Support for survivors and caregivers: See their listing of
National and provincial services and resources

Parkinson's Foundation (800-473-4636) contact@parkinson.org

Frontotemporal
Dementia (FTD)

About frontotemporal dementia

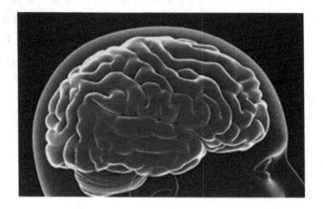

Amyotrophic Lateral Sclerosis(ALS)
All called Lou Gehrig's
Disease

ALS or Lou Gehrig's disease is a rare neurological disease involving the breakdown, and eventual death, of neurons that control voluntary muscles.

The brain loses the ability to initiate and control movement, often resulting in an inability to eat, speak and move, and even breathe.

Approximately 5,000 people in the US are diagnosed with this condition per year, according to the ALS Foundation. There is no known ALS, but doctors do have treatments and therapies that can slow down or ease symptoms for you or a loved one. [13]

---

[13] WebMD www.webmd.com

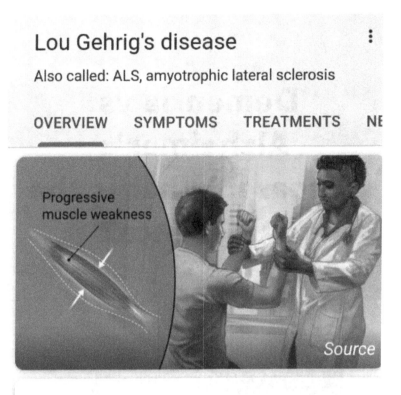

Lou Gehrig's disease ⋮

Also called: ALS, amyotrophic lateral sclerosis

OVERVIEW   SYMPTOMS   TREATMENTS   NE

Progressive muscle weakness

Source

A nervous system disease that weakens muscles and impacts physical function.

In this disease, nerve cells break down, which reduces functionality in the muscles they supply. The cause is unknown.

[14]mayoclinic.org

---

[14] Mayo Clinic is an American nonprofit academic medical center currently based in three major location;
Rochester, Minnesota; Jacksonville, Florida; and Scottsdale, Arizona, focused on integrated patient care, education and research.

Dementia vs. Alzheimer's Disease: What is the Difference?

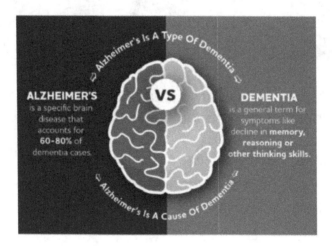

POSSIBLE TREATMENTS

Can Cannabis for CBD oil treat dementia or its symptoms

OIL CBD FOR ALZHEIMER'S

Alzheimer's disease is currently the most commonly developed form of dementia, and it currently affects over five million individuals in the United States. It is possibly the worst type of dementia as it affects one's thinking, memory loss, and also behavior. The negative symptoms of this treacherous disease creep up on you slowly and progressively worsen as time passes until you reach the point where you are no longer able to cope with daily life.

Alzheimer's is very sadly a progressive disease that seems to have no end. In the final stages of the disease, the patient will have lost the ability to have a conversation or react to their environment. It is one of the major causes of death in the elderly, and the expected lifespan after diagnosis is between four and eight years, in some cases.

There is currently no proven cure for Alzheimer's disease, yet there are some treatments available that can help manage the symptoms, and with ongoing research being conducted, medical professionals are hopeful that a cure will be discovered in the near future.

Traditional Treatments for Alzheimer's Disease

The commonly used treatments for Alzheimer's are only capable of temporarily slowing the symptoms of dementia from getting worse. The progression of the disease cannot be stopped entirely, and more than anything, it is a way to improve the quality of lives of patients and their daily lives. Recently, there has been some hope given to members of the Alzheimer's community and their caregivers as it was thought that cannabinoids play a large part in reducing the harmful symptoms of the degenerative disease.

HOW IS CBD OIL USED TO TREAT ALZHEIMER'S?

Cannabinoids and cannabinoid receptors affect a particular part of the brain known as the endocannabinoid system. This intricate internal piece of equipment comprises two receptors: CB1 and CB2 present in each part of the brain, including the hippocampus, which is responsible for our memory function and learning ability. CB2 receptors live in certain immune cells in our brain called microglia. The endocannabinoid system that responds to the signals sent by CBD products is largely responsible for memory, and the hippocampus is the first major part of the body to be destroyed by Alzheimer's disease.

An Introduction to the Endocannabinoid System (What is it?)

Cannabidiol (CBD) is an effective health supplement because they have an endocannabinoid system (ECS) in our body to interact with the cannabis plant, similar to compounds we naturally create in the body.

The relationship between the endocannabinoid system and cannabis is a daily new area of study, although it has piqued the interest of humans for thousands of years. Before the endocannabinoid system was discovered, humans recognized the influence of cannabis on the human body but could not explain the biological process behind it. The search for understanding of the cannabis plant has led researchers to discover the endocannabinoid systems.

What is the Latest News with regards to Treating Alzheimer's with CBD?

Like with helping with the relief of multiple sclerosis, inflammation, cognitive impairment, and chronic pain, a study was conducted focusing on the use of CBD to treat Alzheimer's disease, and it was found that the effects of CBD from the plant Cannabis sativa are indeed capable of effectively treating disorders in the nervous system, including Alzheimer's. Its efficacy comes as a result of cannabinoid's ability to protect nerve cells against damages and deteriorating further swell as its antioxidant properties.

The same research contains new findings that CBD oil can significantly reduce the negative effects that Alzheimer's has on a patient's overall health as well as improving cognitive ability. It seems that Alzheimer's has an effect on a patient's overall health as well as improving cognitive ability. It seems that cannabidiol might actually hold the key to treating and slowing the progression of the fatal disease.

CBD Can Reverse Braining Aging

Other studies from the University of Bonn [Bonn, Germany] show that cannabis reverses aging processes in the brain. A study suggests researchers restore the memory performance of Methuselah mice to a juvenile stage. Memory performance decreases with increasing age. Cannabis can reverse these aging processes in the brain. This was shown in mice by scientists at the University of Bonn with their colleagues at The Hebrew University of Jerusalem (Israel). Old animals were able to regress to the state of two-month-old mice with prolonged, low-dose treatment with a cannabis active ingredient. This opens up new options, for instance, when it comes to treating dementia.

It has been demonstrated how CBD works to reverse the aging process of the brain, which is accelerated by Alzheimer's. It was found that CBD could reverse the aging process of the brain, which is accelerated by Alzheimer's. It was found that CBD could reverse dementia, as well as THC, although this is the element found in cannabis responsible for getting you high. CBD is currently legal in many states and is widely used to treat many kinds of medical conditions.

It Reduces Oxidative Stress

It seems that the beneficial qualities of CBD with regards to treating dementia are never-ending. It has been found to protect against neurotoxicity and help minimize oxidative stress in Alzheimer's patients. And while the need for more factual evidence is apparent, the future looks incredibly bright for CBD as a treatment for Dementia.

FINAL THOUGHTS

CBD oil is making the headlines on a weekly basis as more testimonials emerge from people who have had success using cannabis-based products to treat severe medical conditions. While more research needs to be done on the specific effect of CBD on dementia, there is more than enough evidence to suggest that it could have serious potential as being the sought-after cure for this cruel disease.

While there will always be skeptics opposing certain aspects of the efficacy of medical marijuana, the FACTS DON'T LIE. Neither do the thousands of people across the world that have found that their symptoms of dementia have drastically improved since they started using CBD oil to alleviate the mental fog that is so prevalent in Alzheimer's. 2019 started to be a promising year for the medical marijuana industry, with more states legalizing the herb as well as more medical facilities opting to prescribe natural remedies as opposed to potentially harmful pharmaceuticals.

Supplemental Information

Heart Breaking Interviews From Other Caregivers
To Hear Their Full Interview

These Are Questions That Were Asked

1. _____briefly tell me something about yourself.
2. How long were you a caregiver?
3. When was your loved one/patient diagnosed with Dementia/ Alzheimer's?
4. What other agencies besides the Alzheimer's Association do you seek help for better care for your loved one/patient?
5. Please share some of your difficulties/challenges as a caregiver.
6. Please share some of your most rewarding experiences as a caregiver.
7. Is there anything that you are concerned about that society could do better to help Alzheimer's Caregivers and their loved ones/ patients?
8. *When do you get time for yourself?*

9. What activities do you do to help you stay grounded and happy for yourself?
10. Is there anything you would like to share today we have not discussed today?

Long-term Health Care(LTC) Insurance- is a variety of long -term services to help meet the medical and non-medical needs of people with a chronic illness or disability who cannot care for themselves for long periods. [15]

Daily Care Chart To Do List
Using BOTS

BOT- Means Back On Topic

Chatbots - is a piece of software that can communicate with users in a back-and-forth, conversational way. All kinds of different businesses and organization are using them because they can;

*Automate and scale routine support functions
*Provide education and information in a friendly, digestible style
*Guide shoppers to boost e-commerce sales
*Generate and qualify leads
* Engage users in an exciting new way

Al (Artificial Intelligence) and NLP (National Language Processing)

Chatbots IN HEALTHCARE -are tools used to communicate with patients via text message or voice. Many chatbots are powered by artificial intelligence. In healthcare, caregivers frequently communicate with patients' electronic health to record doctors' notes.

Using Chatbots To Help Caregivers of Alzheimer's Patients

The chatbot mimics conversations between a "helpline" with caregivers using artificial intelligence. The user-centric and always accessible bot

---

[15] **Longtermcare.acl.gov**

helps with solving issues and problems around Alzheimer's the caregiver might encounter

*Chatbots can be used as a backup plan to make sure the caregiver has addressed the needs of the patient for the day.

- Program to use in To Do Chart for daily, weekly, or monthly are example in the chart below;

1. Establish To- Do Chart For Daily Care
   This Chart: List Dates and times, start times and ending time, for example

   a. Bathing
   b. Dressing
   c. Medications
   d. Meals
   e. Bedtime
   f. Interaction Moments, such as;

   1.One-on-one conversations, Reading, Gametime, (puzzles ex. seek-and-find, connect the dots, large colorful puzzles, collect four checker game, arts and crafts, and video games, whatever sparks their interest) Walks/Exercise If possible

2. Always have ample time between each activity

   a. Rushing your loved one may cause
   1. Aggravation
   2. Combative Behavior

3. There possibly will come a time when showering or bathing themselves challenge.

Not wanting to bathe or saying they did bathe, but have not.

Do the following:

    a. Do not confront them negatively. They sometimes can become combative
1. Commonly, say you will help them with bathing
2. Your loved one maybe apprehensive about stepping in the shower or a bathtub. Remember, what used to be is no longer the norm for them
3. Sponge bathes them or one body part at a time with them sitting or standing, whatever is more comfortable to them.
4. The development varies with each individual case.
    a. The development varies with each individual case.

Artificial Intelligence

Artificial Intelligence is a great asset to the health care community, helping caregivers navigate the difficult long days caring for their loved one(s). In the Alzheimer's community and other caregiving communities, we must have an open mind to the future of technology in healthcare. Embracing change and "AI" will help speed up the process to help find a cure and help caregivers team up together for the care of their loved ones.

Scientists are actively looking at Artificial Intelligence for early detection of Alzheimer's before the disease takes over one's life completely. They are looking at the function of the brain early to see if there's a pattern Algorithm that eventually finds a connection in the brain which could detect Alzheimer's disease years prior before it set in to change the person's normal way of life.

Artificial intelligence will help ease the stress, anxiety, and frustration of the caregivers, and the needs are increasingly growing every day. [**According** to the World Alzheimer's +Report on September 20, 2019[16] The report reveals;[the number of people living with dementia is predicted to triple, rising to 152 million by 2050]. Dementia is a term used to describe severe changes in the brain that cause memory loss.[17]

Healthline describes the various types of memory loss;

- Alzheimer's disease is the most common type of dementia with 60 to 80 percent of cases of dementia, according to the Alzheimer's Association
- Vascular dementia is caused by a lack of blood flow to the brain. Vascular dementia can happen as you age and relate to strokes.
- Dementia with Lewy bodies is caused by protein deposits in nerve cells. This interrupts chemical messages in the brain, causing memory loss and disorientation.
- Parkinson's disease dementia might have trouble understanding visual or information and remembering how to do simple daily tasks. They may even have confusing or frightening hallucinations.
- Frontotemporal dementia is described as several types of dementia, all with one thing in common: They affect the front and side parts of the brain, which are the areas that control language and behavior. It's also known as Pick's disease.
- Creutzfeldt-Jakob disease is one of the rarest forms of dementia. Only 1 in 1 million people are diagnosed with it every year. According to the [Alzheimer's Association], CJD progresses very quickly, and people often die within a year of diagnosis. Symptoms of CJD are similar to other forms of dementia. Some people experience agitation, while others suffer from depression. Confusion and loss of memory are also common. CJD affects the body as well, causing twitching and muscle stiffness.
- Wernicke-Korsakoff syndrome- It's technically not a form of dementia. However, symptoms are similar to dementia, and it's

---

[16] **World Alzheimer's Report September 20, 2019**
[17] **Healthline Medically viewed by Timothy J. Legg Ph.D. on June 21-Written by Rachel Nall,**

often classified as dementia. The Wernicke-Korsakoff syndrome can be a result of malnutrition or chronic infections.

- Huntington's disease Impaired movements, such as jerking, difficulty walking, and trouble swallowing. Dementia symptoms: focusing on a task, impulse control problems, trouble speaking clearly, and difficulty learning new things

- Mixed dementia: Many diseases can cause dementia in the late stages. For example, multiple sclerosis can develop dementia. HIV can develop cognitive impairment and dementia, especially if they're not taking antiviral medications.

- Normal-pressure hydrocephalus (NPH) is a condition that causes a person to build excess fluid-filled in the brain's ventricles. The ventricles are fluid-filled spaces designed to cushion a person's brain and spinal cord. They rely on the right amount of fluid to work properly. When the fluid builds up excessively, it places extra pressure on the brain. This can cause damage that leads to dementia symptoms. According to [John Hopkins Medicine], an estimated 5 percent of dementia cases are due to NPH. Some of the potential causes of NPH include injury, bleeding, infection, brain tumor, and previous brain surgeries. However, sometimes, doctors don't know the cause of NPH. Symptoms include poor balance, forgetfulness, changes in mood, depression, frequent falls, and loss of bowel or bladder control.[18]

The care of patients/loved ones sometimes becomes increasingly difficult. Sometimes their behavior changes when you least expect. You are constantly resetting your day to address the possible change in behavior. This is when Artificial Intelligence can smoothly and aggressively help Caregivers, Neurologists, and others in the medical community. By setting up a program to knowingly act on the changed behavior, a Medical Robot could be developed and programmed to identify the various traits of a diagnosed individual with Alzheimer's, Dementia, or other forms of Memory Loss. It could be a great asset moving forward.

---

[18] **Healthline**

Medical Marijuana And Alzheimer

By Healthline

There is some evidence that medical marijuana can help people with Alzheimer's, but researchers say there is a risk, too. Some states are going ahead with plans to allow the use of marijuana by people with Alzheimer's. Health researchers say that might be risky--despite the evidence, there could be some benefits to certain people in some circumstances. The problem is that there just isn't enough of it.

The Minnesota Department of Health (MDH) announced that it would add Alzheimer's disease as a new qualifying condition for the state's medical cannabis program. If a resident has been diagnosed with Alzheimer's, they would be allowed under state law to purchase medical marijuana from a licensed manufacturer.

Alzheimer's would join thirteen other approved conditions, ranging from irritable bowel disease and intractable pain, to HIV and some cancers. At least thirteen other states already allow people with Alzheimer's to use medical marijuana, according to the cannabis website Leafly.

Pennsylvania, one state that doesn't allow it, approved a new way to speed up the addition of new conditions to its medical marijuana list.

In a statement to [**Healthline**], the Alzheimer's Association in the United States said that "marijuana is, essentially, an untested drug in Alzheimer's disease." "Potential effectiveness and safety profile has not been thoroughly evaluated in clinical trials in people with (or at risk for) Alzheimer's. Alzheimer's Association believes that more research in this area is needed.

The Power Of Light

In 2015, neuroscience at The Picower Institute for Learning and Memory at Massachusetts Institute Of Technology found the hippocampal level of beta-amyloid proteins in mice fell by 40-50 percent after only one-hour exposure to 40-hertz light-MedicalNewsToday____

In the Alzheimer's brain, abnormal levels of this naturally occurring protein clump together to form plaques that collect between neurons and disrupt cell function.

The researchers noted that flickering light at 40Hz triggers a tremendous microglia response. Microglia are the brain's immune cells that clear debris and toxic waste, including amyloid.

Flickering Light

In the 2016 study, researchers found a link between gamma and Alzheimer's disease.

Gamma is a type of brainwave that oscillates between 20-50Hz. The 2016 study demonstrated that disruptions to gamma in mice resulted in an increased buildup of plaque protein between brain cells. Plaque protein is a key hallmark of Alzheimer's.

Increased cytokine production

In the new study, the scientist looked in detail at what immune processes were occurring when they exposed the mice to 40 Hz light.

At the same time, a team of scientists from Emory University, Atlanta, GA, were using the research to inform their work on 40 Hz light exposure with humans.

According to Kris Garza, first author of the study, "I'll be running samples from mice in the lab, and around the same time, a colleague will be doing striking similar analysis on patient fluid samples."

The scientist found that when they exposed the mice to 40 Hz light, their brains released more cytokines -a type of protein that communicates with other cells-and the activation of phosphate proteins increased.

This happened rapidly: "We found an increase in cytokines after an hour of stimulation," says Kristie Garza. "We saw phosphoprotein signals after about 15 minutes of flickering."

According to Dr. Singer, "The phosphoproteins showed. It looked as though they were leading, and our hypothesis is that they triggered the release of the cytokines."

In particular, it was the increased release of the cytokine Macrophage Colony-stimulating Factor (M-CSF) that made clear the promotion of microglia. As Dr. Singer notes, "M-CSF was the thing that yelled, Microglia activation!"

According to the co-lead of the study Dr. Levi Wood, the vast majority of cytokines went up, some anti-inflammatory and some inflammatory, and it was a transient response. Often, a transient inflammatory response can promote pathogen clearance; it can promote repair."

"Generally, you think of an inflammatory response as being bad if it's chronic, and this was rapid, and then so, we think that was probably beneficial," adds Dr. Singer.

Biogen Alzheimer's

It's a pretty story in Alzheimer's disease research, with years of flops and setbacks against the memory-wasting disease.

There is a small glimmer of hope (a very, very small glimmer) that Biogen's once-failed, now-resurrected Alzheimer's effort aducanumab can be the first approved med for the condition in more than 15 years.

Biogen has been hinting since the start of the year, with the investors also making the same prediction that a filing with the FDA was 'imminent"; they're at that time four months down the line, and a major global pandemic appears to have scuppered those plans.

A review from life sciences data firm GlobalData said, "the filing and review of Biogen recombinant human monoclonal antibody (mAb) aducanumab is expected to take more time than was estimated." How much time, they didn't know.

GlobalData stated that they do know it will be one of the most controversial drugs to come across the FDA's desk, but they have to wait longer to see how the regulator deals with it.

It's also all too easy to forget just how damaging, life-threatening, and life-changing other diseases and disorders are. But other areas are suffering. Whether Biogen's drug can help Alzheimer's patients or not, GlobalData points out that many trials for the disease are at risk. There aren't many patients to test during a pandemic because they are considered the most vulnerable in a pandemic.

In the U.K; for example, in 2020, everyone over 70 years old has been told to stay home for 12 weeks. Virtual trails can help here, but they come with more challenges for an older population not always used to such technology.

"With many countries putting clinical trial studies on hold, during that time, pharmaceutical companies were shifting their overall priorities away from some current indications toward more "COVID-19" at the time," the firm said in a report.

This put several Alzheimer's Disease (AD) drugs, of which there were 38 in phase 1, 19 in phase 3 and 37 in phase 2, at risk of delay."

Aless Brunello, the senior pharma analyst at GlobalData, said: "Not all pharmaceutical companies had been responding in the same ways to the COVID-19 pandemic. For example, Roche was continuing both enrollment dosing in the company's AD late-stage trial of gantenerumab. On the other hand, Eli Lilly, which had several AD drugs in the pipeline, is halting enrollment and postponing new trails."

He added: "The disruption of important clinical research by the COVID-19 pandemic is linked to the particular vulnerability of older adults.

ACKNOWLEDGMENTS

Dr. Murray Grossman, M.D. Associate Professor of University of Pennsylvania Medical Center, University of Pennsylvania School of Medicine, Department of Neurology, Division of Cognitive Neurology. Dr. Grossman, words cannot express your exemplary care for my husband, John Beckwith.

Dr. Howard Caplan, Neurologist Lankenau Medical Office (location in the year 2002) Wynnwood, PA Neurologist Department. First diagnosed Jay with Dementia with early signs of the onset of Alzheimer's Disease and insisted we get a second opinion from Dr. Grossman. Thank you for your continuous care and concern.

Dr. Bonnie, Gardner, Endocrinologist, treated Jay for Diabetes in Bala Cynwyd. Pa (location in the year 2002) Thank you.

Sarah and Ulysess Cox, my parents, both of you help me with my struggles. Caregiving behind closed doors to protect my privacy at my request. Encouraging me and helping Jay through our journey navigating Alzheimer's Disease. Thank you, I love and miss both of you so much. Rest in peace.

Khadija and Khaleel Dugan, my daughter and son. Thank you both for your patience. There were constant changes in our home, and I know it was very difficult for both of you, but you understand and continually adjust to the changes. Khadija and Khaleel, you are champions in helping me various times with Jay's care, the various chores around the house, and our difficult vacations together as a family. Khaleel learned how to chauffeur and manage the family limo business when Jay could no longer participate in the limo business.

Federick Johnson, my son-in-law, Thank you for stepping in various times of emergencies, driving long or short distances with patience and a smile.

Janet and Thomas James, my twin sister and brother-in-law, whenever I called for help with my husband, both of you were always there. You will ask me what I needed, where to go, or how they could help. At the beginning of Jay's diagnosis, when I was at work, I asked you to check-in on Jay. He was home alone painting, and it was your day off from work. With no hesitation, Janet, you drove there. When you arrived, Jay was so confused and disoriented. You patiently calm him down and call me. Thank you for being there for me.

Jason Brown, my nephew, Thank you for mindlessly stepping in as a Limousine Driver. Chauffeuring and managing Jay on business calls professionally as well as quickly learning to chauffeur clients and effortlessly learning the family limo business when Jay could no longer participate in the business.

Andrea S. (Andy) Thomas and Reginald M. Thomas, my best friend and her husband. Thank you for continually inviting us to your home with all our challenges. Helping out when Jay forgot how to swim in your pool and stopping him when he tried to wander outside during the middle of the night. Thank you both for your prayers, patience, and unconditional friendship.

Lana Sheridan Sr. Administrative Assistant, Family Caregiver Alliance National Center On Caregiving (FCA)

Yolanda Wright, MSW, LMSW Early Stage and Support Group Coordinator, Alzheimer's Association-Greater Maryland Chapter. Thank you for sharing the Greater Maryland Chapter Groups

Edgar Parker, Facilitator of the Alzheimer's Chapter Support at Anne Arundel County AAMC Belcher Pavilion, Annapolis, Maryland. Thanks for giving me the permission to sit in on a few of your meetings, spending time before and after meetings discussing your personal journey, caring, and dedication of the park bench in memory of your wife, simply beautiful. The various processes you do through as a facilitator for a number of years.

Florence Nightingale (asked to remain anonymous) Contributor at the Alzheimer's Chapter Support group. Thank you for sharing your experience as a caregiver of a family member. It was a welcome pleasure hearing your story, engaging the readers and me that we are not alone in our journey as a caregiver of our loved one(s).

Peggy S. Jackson, Facilitator of the M.A.R Alzheimer's Caregivers Support Group,

At Sharon Baptist Church, 1373 N. Stricker St, Baltimore, Maryland. Ms. Jackson, thank you for opening your heart and your doors to help with my book. Your personal experience with Mother's care and other caregivers' experiences in your Alzheimer's community. You helped me realize that I am on the right track, assisting other caregivers too.

Betty J. Whitaker, Contributor from Alzheimer's Caregivers Support Group, Sharon Baptist Church Thank you for sharing your personal experience as the caregiver of your husband with me. It was a pleasure speaking with you. Your relentless care of your husband by you and your daughters was so heartwarming

RESOURCE

AARP -American Association of Retired Person -AARP.org- (formed called American Association of Retired Persons) is a United States-based interest group focusing on issues affecting those over the age of fifty, according to the organization

Alzhemier's Association Greater Chapter Maryland ALZ.org Maryland-provides support
Groups, free education, and online services. They serve the following areas: Allegany, Ann Arundel, Baltimore City, Baltimore County, Caroline, Carroll, Cecil, Dorchester, Frederick, Garrett, Hartford, Howard, Kent, Queen Anne's, Somerset, Talbot, Washington, Wicomico, Worcester

FierceBiotech- is a free daily email newsletter and web resource providing the latest
biotech news, articles, and resources related to clinical trials, drug discovery, FDA
approval and regulation, biotech company deals, and more.

Mayoclinic.org -nonprofit organization committed to clinical practice, education, and
research, providing expert, whole-person care to everyone who needs healing

Heart & Stroke Foundation-is committed to creating awareness around the effects of heart disease and stroke. Through research, advocacy, to eliminate heart disease and stroke and reduce their impact.

Long Term Care.acl.gov-is a range of services and supports you may need to meet your
personal care needs. Most long-term care is not medical, but rather assistance with the basics personal tasks of every life, sometimes called Activities of Daily Living (IADLs)

ACL- Administration For Community Living:acl.gov The Administration for part of the United States Department of Health and Human Services. It is headed by the Administration, who reports directly to the Secretary of Health and Human Services. ACL's Principal Deputy Administrator serves as Senior Advisor to the HHS Secretary for Disability Policy. Community Eldercare Locator call at1-800-677-1116 https:// eldercare.acl.gov

Alzheimer's Caregivers Support Group, Anne Arundel Medical Center, 2001 Medical Parkway Annapolis, Maryland 21401

Alzheimer's Caregivers Support Group M.A.R., Sharon Baptist Church, Stricker and Presstman Streets, Baltimore, Maryland 21217

Alzheimer's Foundation-America AFA, alzfdn.org, 1250 24th St NW, Washington, DC 20037

Alzheimer's Association (2015) Alzheimer's Disease [Facts and Figures]

2020 Alzheimer's Disease Facts and Figures, Home Office: 225 N. Michigan Ave
Floor 17 Chicago, IL 60601

American Heart Association, 217 E Redwood St, #1100, Baltimore, MD 21201

Behavior Risk Factor Surveillance System (BRFSS)- is the nation's premier system of health-related telephone surveys that collect state data about U.S. residents regarding their health-related risk behaviors, chronic health conditions, and use of preventive services.

Biogen Inc.-is an American multinational biotechnology company based in Cambridge, Massachusetts, specializing in the discovery, development, and delivery of therapy for
the treatment of neurological diseases to patients worldwide

Family Caregiver Alliance, National Center on Caregiving, 101 Montgomery Street,
San Francisco, CA 94104

GlobalData - a leading information services company, thousands of clients rely on trusted, timely, and actionable intelligence. Its solutions are designed to provide a daily edge to professionals within corporations, financial institutions, professional services, and government agencies.

Journal Of Internal Medicine /Volume 277, Issue 4
Heart failure And Alzheimer's disease. Wiley Online Library
First published 15 July, 2014
https://doi.org/10.1111/joim.12287

HEMPEMAIL:support@madebyhemp.com

Medicaid.gov

National Institute Aging ADEAR

"Courtesy: National Institute of Aging National Human Genome Research Institute" genome.gov. (NIH) Down Syndrome Research

MedlinePlus MedlinePlus.gov

Massachusetts Institute of Technology-is private research university in Cambridge, Massachusetts

Minnesota Department Of Health (MDH)

National Alliance For AARP (2015) The research was conducted by NAC and AARP Public Policy Institute by Greenwald & Associates, with study direction by Lisa Weber-Raley and Erin Smith.

National Alliance For Caregiving-The Alliance's mission is to be the objective national
resource on family caregiving with the goal of improving the quality of life for families
and care recipients.

National Library of Medicine (NLM), Bethesda, Maryland 20894

November Is Alzheimer's National Family Caregivers Month-contributions of caregivers,
provide them with tools that they need, and continue to advocate for individuals with
mental illness

Penn Medicine Department Of Neurology, 3 West Gate Building, 3400 Spruce Street National Institutes of HealthStreet, Philadelphia, PA 19104-4283

Parkinson's Foundation-makes life better for people with Parkinson's disease by improving care and advance research toward a cure

Picower Institute for Learning and Memory

Pinterest.com - is an American image sharing and social media service designed to enable saving and discovery of information.

RAND Military Caregivers Study-The study focuses on the caregivers of wounded, ill and injured military service members and veterans. Funded by the Elizabeth Dole Foundation, the study aims to quantify military caregivers' needs and examine existing policies and programs for meeting them.

United Health Foundation (2010)

USA.gov

United States Census Bureau- Provided American Counts for Caregivers Alliance
National Center on Caregiving

U.S. National Institutes of Health

University of Eastern Finland

WebMD News from HealthDay
WebMD Medical References

World Alzheimer's Day is on 21 September each year. Raise awareness and challenge the stigma that surrounds dementia

World Alzheimer's Disease International Report 2019
www.alz.co.uk/worldreport2019

Simple Home Test The Caregiver Observes
With Beginning Stages of Member Challenges

1. Forgetting a simple task that otherwise is normal to him/her.
    a. Laundry
    b. Bathing
    c. Use the toilet

2. Now uninterested
    a. Sports
    b. Vacations
    c. Person hobbies that use to enjoy
    d. Communicating with others (Communication is sometimes difficult)

3. All of a sudden, constantly misplacing personal items
    a. Keys
    b. Something that used to be of value to them
    c. Money

4. Sense of direction is confusing, walking, driving, or finding an area/place that used to be familiar.

5. Counting funds

6. Household finances are suddenly confusing

7. Presenting him/her to remember 3 simple objects. Afterward, have them count backward from 100 to 90. Next, ask them to recall the 3 objects. (The outcome is unpredictable)Possibly can't finish the task

8. Writing a simple letter

9. Pleasurable activities him/her no longer interested

10. Confusion in the kitchen
    a. Preparing favorite recipes no longer can prepare
    b. Leaving the stove on
    c. Not placing items in the kitchen back to their original place
        1. Food in the refrigerator
        2. Utensils
        3. Cabinets